Ann Lyon

Wine - ALVARINHO 2000

503

THOMAS COOK
Traveller

ALGARVE

BY
SUSIE BOULTON, JOE STAINES,
SARAH LE TELLIER, MARTIN SYMINGTON

Produced by AA Publishing

Written by Susie Boulton, Joe Staines, Sarah Le Tellier, Martin Symington

Edited, designed and produced by AA Publishing. Maps © Automobile Association Developments Ltd 1993, 1999

Distributed in the United Kingdom by AA Publishing, Norfolk House, Priestley Road, Basingstoke, Hampshire, RG24 9NY.

The contents of this publication are believed correct at the time of printing. Nevertheless, the publishers cannot accept responsibility for errors or omissions, or for changes in details given. Assessments of attractions, hotels, restaurants and so forth are based upon the author's own experience and, therefore, descriptions given in this guide necessarily contain an element of subjective opinion which may not reflect the publishers' opinion or dictate a reader's own experiences on another occasion.

We have tried to ensure accuracy in this guide, but things do change and we would be grateful if readers would advise us of any inaccuracies they may encounter.

First published 1993
Revised second edition 1995; Reprinted 1997 and January 1998
Revised third edition 1999; Reprinted 1999 and August 2000
© Automobile Association Developments Ltd 1993, 1995, 1999

A CIP catalogue record for this book is available from the British Library.

ISBN 0 7495 1938 X

Published by AA Publishing (a trading name of Automobile Association Developments Limited, whose registered office is Norfolk House, Priestley Road, Basingstoke, Hampshire RG24 9NY. Registered number 1878835) and the Thomas Cook Group Ltd.

Colour separation: BTB Colour Reproduction, Whitchurch, Hampshire
Printed by Edicoes ASA, Oporto, Portugal
Front cover: *Praia da Luz;* Title page: *The Ponta da Piedade;* Above: *Typical church architecture*
AA World Travel Guides publish nearly 300 guidebooks to a full range of cities, countries and regions across the world. Find out more about AA Publishing and the wide range of services the AA provides by visiting our Web site at www.theaa.co.uk.

Contents

Introduction

*P*ortugal is the westernmost country of mainland Europe, with over 800km of coastline facing the vast expanse of the Atlantic Ocean. The sea has dominated Portugal's history, from the great voyages of discovery in the late 15th century to the fleets of fishermen who still journey as far as Newfoundland and Greenland in search of their catch.

Moorish legacy

For such a small country, Portugal is remarkably varied, and there is a marked difference between the north and the south. The character of southern Portugal has been influenced by its proximity to Africa, and by successive visitors from the Mediterranean – Phoenicians, Romans and Moors – who have all left their distinctive mark. In particular the Moorish occupation of the south, which began in AD 711 and lasted right up until 1249, had a lasting effect on the region's architecture, crafts, agriculture and arts.

Gaily painted fishing boats are a characteristic feature of the Algarve

Today visitors from all over the world flock to the thin strip of Portugal's southern coast that makes up the Algarve. Even with the transforming effect of recent tourist development, this region retains its appeal. It enjoys an equable climate, with hardly any summer rain, and long stretches of perfect sandy beach, not to mention good, simple food and a warm and welcoming people. For those for whom beach life is not an attraction, there is much else to discover in the south. The huge plains of the Alentejo remain underexplored by visitors; like the Algarve, it erupts into a colourful riot of wild flowers between February and June. It also possesses a wealth of historical monuments and works of art, many of them concentrated in the exquisite and ancient city of Évora. Finally, for those fed up with the bustle of modern life, the isolated villages along the Spanish border provide the perfect escape.

SOUTHERN PORTUGAL QUOTES

'Where the land ends and the sea begins...'
Luís de Camões, from *The Lusiads* (1572)

'In the sea off Lusitania acorn-bearing oaks grow, upon which the tunnies feed and fatten themselves...'
Polybius, from the *Histories* (c150 BC)

'Everywhere the children regard us with a savage confidence. Here (Lagos) they are quite troublesome in impudence. How do the Portuguese live...? Fish and pulse and bread!! Mutton they dislike even when good. At Faro it is often called goat's flesh to make it saleable.'
Robert Southey, from his *Portuguese Journal* (1800–01)

A typical Algarvian beach

'It was evening; herds of black goats, driven by little boys and girls in great straw hats, tripped along the dusty road; small donkeys ambled home, their panniers full of water pots or vegetables or turf; the smell of flowers and sticky fig leaves drifted on the warm air.'
Rose Macaulay on the Algarve, from *Fabled Shore* (1949)

'I passed the day succeeding my arrival principally in examining the town (Évora) and its environs, and as I strolled about, entered into conversation with various people that I met; several of these were of the middle class... When I spoke of religion, they exhibited the utmost apathy for the subject, and making their bows, left me as soon as possible.'
George Borrow, from *The Bible in Spain* (1843)

'The fields in these days of mid-June had the first golden ears of ripe corn, waving and fat, which the breeze bends down in groups of gracious welcome. On both sides, between sheaves piled up anyhow, the scarlet of the poppies was laughing like the lips of ardent girls.'
José Fialho de Almeida on the Alentejo, from *Aves Migradoras* (1893)

History

2nd millennium BC
Iberian tribes arrive in the peninsula.
Around 1000 BC
Phoenicians set up trading stations and settlements in the Algarve.
Around 700 BC
Invasion of Celtic settlers who later intermarry with the Iberians to become Celtiberians.
Around 210 BC
Occupation by the Romans. The Algarve area, along with northwest Africa, is named *Cyneticum;* the native population is known as the *Conii.*
Around 27 BC
Caesar Augustus pacifies the peninsula after a series of uprisings by the native population. The province south of the Douro river is named Lusitania.
Around AD **200**
Introduction of Christianity.
Around 409
The peninsula is invaded by the Suevi, the Vandals and the Alani – barbarian tribes from central Europe.
415
Visigoths invade the peninsula, driving out the Vandals and Alani and eventually taking over the Suevi capital, Toledo.
711
A large Muslim army of Berbers and Arabs, known collectively as Moors, conquers the peninsula following a dispute over the Visigothic succession. The lands west of the Guadiana river, the area now known as the Algarve and the Alentejo, are named *al-Gharb al-Andalus* ('the west of Andalus') and occupied mainly by Yemenites who introduce irrigation, rice-fields and fruit-farms.

1086
The peninsula is invaded by the Almoravides of North Africa seeking to combat the Christian Reconquest.
1139
Afonso Henriques defeats a Muslim army at Campo Ourique in the Alentejo and declares himself King of Portugal.
1147
Lisbon is recaptured from the Muslims.
1173
The remains of St Vincent (who died in the 4th century to become the peninsula's first martyr) are taken from Cape St Vincent to Lisbon, to symbolise that city's liberation from Muslim rule.
1189
King Sancho I of Portugal captures Silves, the Moorish capital of the Algarve, but only holds it for two years.
1249
King Afonso III of Portugal completes the reconquest of the Algarve, finally ending Moorish rule, but his claim to sovereignty is challenged by Castile.
1385
A Castilian army invades Portugal but is routed at the Battle of Aljubarrota. The leader of the victorious Portuguese army is crowned King João I. He marries John of Gaunt's daughter, Philippa, establishing the long-standing alliance between England and Portugal.
1415
Portuguese imperial expansion begins with the capture of Ceuta in Morocco.
1418
Prince Henry 'the Navigator' (son of King João I) becomes governor of the Algarve and sponsors several voyages of discovery.

1496
Portuguese Jews are forcibly converted to Christianity or expelled.
1498
Vasco da Gama sails to India via the southern tip of Africa.
1500
Pedro Alvares Cabral reaches Brazil.
1578
King Sebastião leads Portugal into a disastrous crusade against the Moors. He is killed, and the Portuguese army is annihilated by the Moroccans at the battle of Alcácer-Quibir.
1580
King Philip II of Spain, taking advantage of Portugal's weakness, claims the Portuguese throne and unites the two kingdoms.
1587
Sir Francis Drake attacks Lagos and Sagres in the war against the Spanish. In the process, the house and navigational school of Henry the Navigator are both destroyed.
1596
The Earl of Essex sacks Faro, seizing the Bishop's library which is removed to the Bodleian Library in Oxford, England.
1637
Riots in the Algarve and the Alentejo against Spanish rule.
1640
The Duke of Bragança restores Portuguese independence and is crowned King João IV following an uprising against the Spanish.
1755
An earthquake destroys Lisbon along with much of the Algarve and the Alentejo.
1807
Napoleon's army invades Portugal for failing to declare war on Britain. The Portuguese royal family flees to Brazil.

1808–11
The Peninsula War. British and Portuguese troops under Wellington drive the French out of Portugal.
1832–33
The War of the Two Brothers. The Absolutist Pedro IV defeats his younger brother, the Liberal Miguel, with help from the British.
1889
The Lisbon to Algarve railway is opened.
1908
Republican activists assassinate King Carlos I in Lisbon.
1910
The Republican Revolution: King Manuel II is forced to abdicate, bringing an end to the monarchy.
1933
After 23 years of turmoil and economic decline, Prime Minister Salazar establishes the totalitarian 'New State'. Strikes and all forms of opposition are banned.
1974
A group of radical army officers carry out a bloodless coup, known as the 'Carnation Revolution', because the soldiers carry flowers in their rifle barrels. A new democratic constitution is drawn up and elections, held the following year, lead to victory for the Socialist-led government of Prime Minister Soares.
1975
The Portuguese colonies of Mozambique, Angola and East Timor are given their independence.
1986
Portugal joins the European Community and Soares becomes the first civilian (ie non-military) President of Portugal.
1998
Last World Exposition of the 20th century takes place in Lisbon.

Geography

*P*ortugal, occupying the western strip of the Iberian peninsula, looks small and modest on the map, especially by comparison with neighbouring Spain. Indeed, Portugal's land area (88,944sq km) takes up less than one-fifth of the peninsula and yet it still manages to be a country of astonishing diversity, both in its physical characteristics and in its differing ways of life.

Portugal is bounded to the north and the east by Spain and to the south and the west by the Atlantic Ocean. It is a continuation of the Iberian Meseta, or high tableland, which slopes gradually down to the sea in the south. The highest mountain range is the Serra da Estrêla, in the middle of the country, which rises to 2,000m. The climate is extremely temperate with most of the low rainfall occurring in winter and more heavily in the north than in the south.

THE ALGARVE

The Algarve is the southernmost region of Portugal. It is separated from Spain, to the east, by the Guadiana river and from the Alentejo region, to the north, by two mountain ranges, the Serra de Monchique and the Serra do Caldeirão. These mountains, which cover almost two-thirds of the region, are made up of carboniferous shale which disintegrates

The view from the summit of Fóia

easily. Heather, *cistus* (rock rose) and gorse grow here but serious cultivation is practically impossible due to erosion; apart from the spa of Caldas de Monchique, this area is rarely visited.

Immediately to the south of the mountains is a limestone zone which runs across the region from east to west known as the Barrocal, a name that suggests wasteland as much as limestone. In fact much of the Barrocal is cultivated; almonds, figs, olives and carob – all introduced by the Moors – grow here in abundance and are an important part of the Algarvian economy.

Of course, most visitors to the Algarve come for the coast, the western half of which, from Cabo de São Vicente (Cape St Vincent) to Faro, is famous for its golden cliffs, full of caves and crevices, and its small sheltered beaches. The eastern half, called the Sotavento

The map below uses the international symbol Ⓔ to indicate Spain.

and stretching from Faro to Vila Real de Santo António, has a less dramatic, but equally sun-drenched, succession of sandy beaches. Tourism now vies with fishing as the major industry of the area, but the centuries-old pursuit of the sardine and the tuna still thrives.

THE ALENTEJO

This region, north of the Algarve, consists of one vast and level plain, except for the mountains of the Serra de Marvão and the Serra de São Mamede in the northeast. Most of the land is divided into large estates, or *latifundios,* centred around a farm complex called a *monte.* The region has no really big towns or cities. Évora and Beja both have populations of about 175,000.

Arable farming predominates, but there is also much unfarmed heathland as well as extensive cork oak forests; processing of the bark is an important industry, both here and in the Algarve. Traditional, but increasingly uncommon, are the great flocks of sheep – and sometimes pigs – watched over by herdsman who wear large and all-enveloping sheepskin capes in winter.

Centuries of exploitation by (often absentee) landlords has made the *alentejanos* the most politically radical and anti-clerical of all the Portuguese. The Alentejo has been consistent in its support of the Communist Party. Despite land reforms, following the Carnation Revolution of 1974, this is still an economically depressed region with a high level of unemployment. It is famed, however, for being meticulously clean and tidy and the villagers of the region take pride in their simple lime-washed houses, which they decorate with borders of ochre or pale grey.

Flora

*P*ortugal might be on the Atlantic coast, but the south, at least, has more of a Mediterranean climate, with the result that the area has a particularly rich flora. With most visitors firmly fixated on the possibilities of sun and sand, few stop to notice the magnificent array of literally thousands of species of wild flowers that cram themselves into every nook and cranny, clinging precariously to dunes and rocky cliff faces, huddling into ditches and marshes and lining every roadside verge. From February to June, the entire landscape turns into a blaze of colour as the plants rush to flower and set seed before the onset of the intense summer heat. By the start of the main tourist season, in July and August, the land is once again parched and brown, while the remaining foliage looks withered and dusty.

Coastal plants

Of all the coastal plants, perhaps the most common is the *cistus* or rock rose, found here in a dozen different forms, from scrubby bush to ground creeper; the leaves are shiny, waxy, sticky or hairy, all different ways of trapping the small amounts of moisture available. Among the most common species are

The morning glory vine, so called because the flowers open at dawn

Cistus phalhinhae, a low-growing plant with shiny leaves and small, frilly pure-white flowers; *Cistus ladanifer,* commonly known as gum cistus, a bush with sticky leaves and white flowers with crimson blotches; *Cistus salviifolius,* which has large, furry leaves, similar to sage; and *Cistus albidus,* which has grey leaves and a rich magenta flower.

On the beaches, other common plants include sea-heath and matted sea knotgrass, bushy sea spurge and sea stocks, thrift *(Armeria pungens),* which has tall pink flowers, and cream-flowered milk vetch *(Astragalus massiliensis),* nicknamed the 'hedgehog plant' because of its rounded, spiky clumps. Above all, keep an eye out for the bizarre, parasitic saltmarsh broomrape *(Cistanche phelypea),* which pokes out of the bare sand like a yellow-flowered asparagus stalk.

The *maquis*

As you head inland, you find yourself wrapped in the heady fragrance of the Mediterranean-style scrubland which covers many of the infertile hills. Herbs

such as rosemary, thyme, sage and lavender grow alongside broom and heather. Shade is provided by conifers such as juniper, joint, umbrella, Aleppo and stone pines, while wild irises, squills, tassel hyacinths and catchfly *(Silene colorata)* add patches of bright colour. Hunt carefully among the rocks and you can find several different species of shy bee orchid *(Ophrys)* family, such as sawfly, yellow bee, tongue, bug and naked man. The thorny Judas Tree, the luxurious oleander, and the carob *(Ceratonia siliqua)* are all old indigenous species that somehow managed to avoid destruction during successive Ice Ages. Of them all, look out in particular for the carob, also known as the locust tree. An evergreen with large, dark-green leathery leaves, it normally grows as a dense bush about 5m high. It flowers in autumn, but its pendulous pods, up to 20cm long, can be seen at all times of the year. Known by the Arabs as *kirat*, it was the weight of the carob bean which set the carat standard used ever since as a measure for diamonds and other precious stones. Today, it is harvested commercially for use as a gum for papermaking, as a food stabiliser, as cattle feed and, by humans, as a slightly healthier substitute for chocolate.

The fiery flowers of the hibiscus

Fields, hills and woodlands

Although much of the Alentejo consists of rolling prairie, given over largely to wheat production, it is as yet virtually untouched by herbicides and hundreds of species of native field flowers still thrive. At times you can almost imagine that the verges are on fire, with tall tongues of yellow lupins, the flickering richness of bright orange marigolds and poppies glowing scarlet as embers. The cultivated trees, such as almonds, olives, figs, oranges and lemons, are themselves a wonderful sight in full flower, but they also provide shelter for a host of shade-loving wild flowers.

In the volcanic mountains that separate the Algarve from the Alentejo, the vegetation is lusher and greener. Rhododendrons run wild beside the road, along with the extraordinary strawberry tree, while behind are thick groves of beech, chestnut, birch, maple and several different species of oak. Predominant among these are the evergreen, tauzin and, above all, the cork oak, an indigenous tree, left much to its own devices except at harvest time.

Politics

*P*ortugal ceased to be a monarchy in 1910 after the bloodless Republican Revolution forced the last king, Manuel II, into exile in Britain. The Republican party's main target, after the monarchy, was the power of the Catholic Church, which it effectively outlawed. Universal male suffrage was introduced in 1911 and a new constitution drawn up.

However, divisions within the party rapidly developed, the much-needed land reforms failed to materialise and stable government seemed an impossibility. In 1926, after 45 governments in 16 years, a military coup took place. Under President Carmona, parliament was suspended, strikes were banned and censorship was introduced. Then, in 1928, Antonio Salazar, Professor of Economics at Coimbra University, was appointed Minister of Finance.

The new state

Salazar's main task was to remedy the country's disastrous economic situation, caused by a substantial national debt. This he more or less achieved by pursuing an extreme monetarist policy, virtually cutting all public spending. In 1930 he founded the National Union party and two years later he became Prime Minister, a position he held until he suffered a stroke, causing his retirement, in 1968.

The Estado Novo or 'New State' that he presided over was a right-wing

The Câmara Municipal (Town Hall), Faro

dictatorship modelled on Italian Fascism. It was less overtly militaristic and expansionist than other fascist regimes, but no less brutal in the suppression of its opponents through its secret police force, the PIDE. Strikes and trade unions were banned, only one political party was permitted and suffrage was limited. At the same time the modernisation of the country's industry and infrastructure remained slow and half-hearted, with Portugal remaining dependent on its colonies for many commodities and raw materials.

The Carnation Revolution

Despite the moderate reforms of Salazar's successor, Caetano, increasing dissatisfaction with the colonial wars in Africa led a group of radical army officers to organise a revolution. On 25 April, 1974, the Armed Forces Movement (MFA), supported by Communist and Socialist parties, took control of Lisbon. Spontaneous popular support followed, with demonstrators placing red carnations in the soldier's guns. A Revolutionary Council was set up following an attempted military counter-coup and a year later the first free elections, since 1926, were held.

The Socialist Party (PS) won 38 per cent of the vote and the Popular Democrats (PPD) were next with 26 per cent. A coalition government introduced a programme of decolonisation, nationalisation and land reform, turning the vast estates of the south into workers' co-operatives. A Socialist constitution, introduced in 1976, established Portugal as a republican parliamentary democracy but, over the next 10 years, the failure by any party to win an overall majority led to uneasy alliances and increasing economic instability.

Since 1976, elections have become an almost annual event in Portugal

Recent developments

In 1987, Aníbal Cavaco Silva, the leader of the right-of-centre Social Democratic Party (PSD) became the first Prime Minister since 1974 to win a clear majority in parliament. As a result his government has been able to introduce legislation re-privatising many sectors of the economy.

Attempts to reform labour laws met with public opposition and, initially, the presidential veto. Under the Portuguese constitution new legislation must not only be passed by the National Assembly, it must also be approved by a constitutional court and accepted by the President. Since 1986, the President, the former Socialist leader Mário Soares, has acted as a check on the somewhat authoritarian style of Cavaco Silva. Nevertheless, laws facilitating the dismissal of workers were finally passed in 1988 and revisions to the constitution, ridding it of its original socialist programme, became law in 1989.

Culture

*S*outhern Portugal – south of the River Tejo (Tagus) – looks and feels utterly different from the north. This is largely due to the legacy of the Moors whose presence in the region lasted over five centuries. Monuments to their culture are fewer and less spectacular than in neighbouring Andalucia; they include the castle at Silves, parts of a mosque at Mértola and the remains of the Moorish quarter at Moura. But the domestic architecture of the Algarve and the Alentejo has a distinctively North African character – not just in the squareness of the buildings and their whitewashed exteriors, but also in the ornate filigree chimneys of the Algarve and the distinctive roof terraces of Olhão, and everywhere are the decorated glazed tiles called *azulejos*. The Moors also left their mark on the land with the introduction of rice, figs and, of course, the almond which blossoms so gloriously in February.

Manueline architecture

Southern Portugal is not known primarily for the quality of its church architecture, but for one short period, in the late 15th and 16th centuries, there came a burst of building activity that created a new and unique style.

Elsewhere in Europe, High Gothic art reached its pinnacle as the Renaissance swung into action in Italy. The Portuguese were hot on the trail of new colonies and trade routes; and in Spain, Ferdinand and Isabel (the 'Catholic Monarchs') flung the last of the Moors off the Iberian peninsula, along with 250,000 Jews, topping off their actions by letting loose the Inquisition.

Their influence spread across the border, and this became the great age of Christian fervour. As town after town rushed to build ever more glorious churches, Manueline architecture was born, named after King Manuel I, who reigned from 1490 to 1520.

In shape, the church remained basically Gothic, but ceilings became even higher and the arches widened. Above all, the decorative themes changed, becoming more lavish and less overtly religious. With the whole country peering over the horizon, nautical motifs became increasingly prominent – with twisted columns rising to corded arches and stars, globes, knots and anchors appearing on bosses and portals – while doors and windows were garlanded with laurel leaves, roses, poppies and even artichokes.

Arts and crafts

Since the advent of tourism many traditional crafts, previously on the verge of extinction, have been revived and there is a wealth of *artesanato* shops and stalls to choose from. Much of the art and craft on sale is genuine local fare but there is also much that is mass-produced, masquerading as handicraft, especially in the Algarve.

The Alentejo

Arraiolos, to the north of Évora, is famed for its carpets. The designs consist of

formalised flowers or animals, made up with an unusual cross-stitch, and natural dyes are used, which mellow with age. In Estremoz, naïve ceramic figurines (*boneços de Estremoz*) are made, often of saints or historical characters. The museum there contains a workshop that makes reproductions of old examples. It also has a series of typical Alentejan rooms with hand-painted furniture.

Unaccompanied male voice choirs are another of the region's notable and thriving artistic traditions. Their songs tell of the hardship and toil of working the land, in melancholy but stirring three- or four-part harmony.

The Algarve

Though neither region has a particular local costume, the women in the mountains of the Algarve wear large black woollen shawls. Weaving is

Ornate basketware is a speciality of the mountain village of Loulé

widespread; rugs, shawls, bedspreads and donkey saddlebags are available, most plentifully in Silves.

Lacework and crocheting were once common handicrafts, and the women of Azinhal were famous for the delicacy of their lace, but the skill has now almost entirely died out. Basketry has not disappeared and a variety of types are made throughout the region. The village of Odeleite, near the Guadiana river, is still a centre for baskets made of split cane. Baskets can also be found at Loulé, though this town is better known for its coppersmiths; they make a wide range of pots and pans, including the *cataplana,* a pan made of two halves which are clipped together when cooking.

TOURIST BOOM

Holiday resorts and apartment blocks now litter the Algarve's stunning coastline, but fishing communities still thrive, supplying sardines to local cafés and markets

Thirty years ago the pleasures of the Algarve were a well-kept secret. This was a region of sleepy fishing villages, where the sight of a stranger would cause intense curiosity. In 1965, when Faro airport was opened, there were just three first-class hotels, and these included the state-run *pousada* in Sagres.

Under the Salazar regime planning controls were very strict so that, though tourism grew substantially before 1974, the real boom did not begin until after the Revolution, reaching a peak in the mid-1980s. Portuguese politicians did not seem to learn much from the horrors of the Spanish Costa del Sol and many crude and nasty developments have been allowed.

Legislation has been introduced in an attempt to prevent areas from becoming completely anglicised, by insisting that there are always signs written in Portuguese. However, attempts by the authorities to encourage more 'quality tourism', by raising prices, resulted in a temporary drop in the number of visitors of almost 10 per cent. Optimism prevails though: Faro airport has been enlarged and the main east/west motorway, the N125, now almost covers the entire width of the Algarve region.

The Alentejo remains relatively under-developed as a tourist area. The supposed monotony of its landscape seems to deter many visitors. Évora, more beautiful than any city in the Algarve, is rarely crowded except for religious festivals. The coast, too, has its critics. It faces the full thrust of the Atlantic and so can be windswept and occasionally dangerous.

Even so, the Alentejo has numerous sandy beaches which remain fairly empty by comparison with the Algarve. In recent years the Serra de Marvão area has become increasingly popular and Turismo de Habitação accommodation has been developed near by, as well as facilities for watersports at several of the local reservoirs.

First Steps

WHAT TO FIND AND WHERE

Beaches

The beaches of the Algarve, in spite of mass tourism, remain some of the most beautiful in Europe. Unfortunately the best, including the famous Praia da Rocha, are often the most over-developed. Remember that there will be less crowding the further you move away from the main beach of any resort. Fishing boats, plus crew, can be hired at several harbours, either for sightseeing or for fishing. For comparative emptiness try the Alentejan coast, especially between Vila Nova de Milfontes and Zambujeiro do Mar.

The curiously shaped rocks and bays of the Praia do Camilo

Castles

To consolidate the Christian Reconquest of Portugal, King Dinis I (1299–1325) embarked on a programme of castle building. Many of these form a line along the Guadiana river, the natural border with Spain. Several, including those at Alcoutim and Terena, are situated in or near quiet, picturesque villages.

Flowers

Spring comes early in the south and from February through to June there is an explosion of many-coloured blossoms, more plentiful in the Algarve than in the Alentejo. The pink and white almond blossom in February is particularly spectacular and by April most of the region's wild flowers are blooming. It has been estimated that the native flora consists of over 1,200 species.

Monuments

The greatest concentration of prehistoric remains is to be found in the countryside surrounding the beautiful medieval hilltown of Monsaraz. Here there are several standing stones, probably used in Celtic fertility rituals.

The Alentejo has more to offer architecturally than the Algarve. Évora has a rich profusion of styles, including a Roman temple and the medieval cathedral. Several prehistoric dolmens can be found near by. Adobe churches – made from mud bricks dried in the sun – can also be found in the Alentejo, for example at Évora and Beja.

Mountains

The Serra de Monchique is the most fertile and accessible of the Algarvian mountains, and a visit to the spa of

Évora's Roman temple and cathedral

Caldas de Monchique and the town of Monchique makes a good contrast to the bustle of the beach.

In the Serra de São Mamede, in the Alto Alentejo, the fortress towns of Portalegre, Marvão and Castelo de Vide provide wonderful views into Spain and, on clear days, as far as the Serra da Estrela in the north.

Sport

The Algarve has an increasing number of sports facilities. Golf has proved to be very popular, with demand outnumbering courses, despite the expense. The Quinta do Lago and Penina courses are the best and most exclusive in Portugal.

Facilities for watersports, such as windsurfing, waterskiing, sailing and diving, are available all along the Algarve coast and in the Alentejo at Vila Nova de Milfontes. Recently facilities have sprung up at some of the inland reservoirs. There is a large marina at Vilamoura where yachts and motor boats can be hired.

The People

*T*he Portuguese are not as outgoing as the Spanish, and this is especially true of the Alentejans, but on the whole they are extremely friendly and polite. In remoter areas, staring at strangers is a sign of curiosity and is not meant aggressively. People are very helpful when their assistance is sought. In those parts of the Algarve most transformed by tourism, a certain brusqueness is not uncommon.

Dress
Though more relaxed in the south, attitudes to dress are quite conservative. Professional people always dress well. For men this means that jacket and tie are *de rigueur,* an attitude which applies to foreigners only in some first-class hotels. Women should not expose too much when visiting churches.

Driving
Portugal has one of the worst records for accidents in Europe. Dangerous driving, especially foolhardy overtaking, is particularly prevalent on motorways.

Football
Football is a national obsession, even though the national side has not done well for many years. There is a daily newspaper, *Bola,* given over entirely to football news. Attending a game is an easy-going, family affair, though none of the top clubs come from the south.

Greetings
It is standard for men to greet each other with a handshake. Women greeting male or female friends usually do so with a kiss on both cheeks, a custom not extended to strangers.

Language
The Portuguese language is not difficult

Traditional festive costume

The young take pride in their dress

to learn but its nasal sounds are difficult to pronounce and even more so to understand (see **Practical Guide**, page 183). Making an attempt to speak the language will be appreciated but many Portuguese speak good English.

Lifestyle

The Portuguese enjoy a siesta period in the afternoon to avoid the midday heat. It is also popular to take an evening stroll around town, a pastime which all members of the family take part in.

Manners

People expect to be treated with respect and courtesy. It is regarded as impolite to stretch or yawn in public.

Patriotism

The Portuguese are intensely proud of the achievements of their country. Internationally renowned Portuguese, from marathon runner Rosa Mota to singer Amália Rodrigues, are spoken of with affection. It is not a good idea to be critical unless speaking to someone you know well. There is a certain mild animosity towards the Spanish, who are seen as overbearing and patronising.

Religion

The majority of the population is Roman Catholic but religious observation is much less strict in the south than in the north of Portugal.

Smoking and spitting

There is a lot of heavy smoking in Portugal and less of an anti-smoking movement than in some countries. It is, however, perfectly acceptable to ask someone to refrain from smoking in a restaurant. Among men, noisy spitting in the street is also extremely commonplace.

Women

There are no particular problems for women travelling alone in Portugal, although it is strongly advisable not to hitch-hike. Portuguese society is not as liberal as that of some European countries and women may give the wrong impression by drawing attention to themselves in this way.

Passing the time of day – a chance to catch up with the latest

Praia da Marinha

This gentle walk of 5km combines quiet lanes with one of the most dramatic sections of the Algarve coast, from the sandy Praia da Marinha to the tiny fishing village of Benagil. There are several cafés and restaurants along the route, and you could extend your walk along unmarked, but well-defined clifftop paths in either direction – east to the clifftop chapel of Senhora da Rocha or west to the Praia do Carvalho and Carvoeiro. *Allow 2 hours.*

The start of the walk can be approached from either Carvoeiro or the N125. West of Porches, midway between Portimão and Albufeira, take the turning opposite the International School. Facing the sea (with the restaurants O Rustico and Brasserie Marina behind you), the building on the hill to the left is a wine factory (Fábrica Vinho): take the lane straight ahead, signposted Praia da Marinha.

1 PRAIA DA MARINHA

In spring the verges and low stone walls along this lane are dotted with wild flowers and the almond trees are in full pink and white blossom. After 1km, passing a small group of houses, the road finishes at a large car-park, where the house on the left has a particularly fine almond tree. To the left a well-maintained stepped path leads past banks of cacti to the beach at Marinha – very popular in summer when you can eat hot or cold snacks on the wooden deck of its restaurant.

Returning to the car-park, take the path leading west, across the cliffs, towards Benagil.

2 THE PATH TO BENAGIL

In its early stretches, the sandstone cliffs have been eroded into unusual ridges; it is possible to walk out to the point overlooking the sea, but great care should be taken, since the cliff edges are extremely friable, and you may prefer to leave it to the seagulls. The next section is perhaps the most impressive – looking back towards Marinha you will see a beaches and caves along the coast.

One beach which you can reach on foot is the Praia do Carvalho. Climb up to the other side of Benagil, where there are several more cafés and restaurants, and along the headland; the beach entrance is down a flight of steps cut into a tunnel in the rock. A single rock stack stands at the centre of this curved bay of deeply shelving sand and, on the far side, steps have been cut into the soft cliff face. In spring it can be deserted; in summer a beach café sells custard-filled doughnuts *(bolos)* and the sand is lined with sunbeds and parasols.

The lane back from Benagil to the car-park climbs past the post office and two more restaurants. It then passes scattered cottages where the old Algarve, of small plots of vines and a few hens, stands side by side with modern villas before returning to the junction at Brasserie Marina. On the lane leading to the wine factory stands a handsome, decaying Algarvian house.

Ochre cliffs and stacks between Praia da Marinha and Benagil

solitary white villa sitting on the headland, with layers of ochre cliffs and stacks between. You can hear, but not always see, the waves crashing against the cliffs below you on to small, inaccessible beaches and into caves and blowholes.

Follow the path as it turns inland to cross a small, green valley and then climb up the other side to rejoin the cliffs.

3 BENAGIL

The headlands towards Benagil are broader, although the village itself remains hidden until the path turns inland and down a flight of steps next to the post office *(Correio)*. You can take the steep road left, down to the small beach and fishing harbour. From here you can take one of the small boats that leave regularly in summer to tour the

Caves eroded by the waves in the soft cliff face at Benagil

São Brás to Estói

This circular motor tour takes in a clutch of churches, the Roman ruins at Milreu and the remarkable rococo palace at Estói. The tour is 34km long and the suggested extension east will add 28km. Note that the main sites on this tour are closed on Mondays. *Allow 3 hours.*

Start in São Brás de Alportel, 17km north of Faro.

1 SÃO BRÁS

São Brás lies well away from the usual tourist circuits in the Barrocal, the limestone zone which lies between the coast and the inland mountains. It has an interesting ethnographic museum. The large parish church, in the square called Largo da Igreja, has an elegant classical façade and bell tower, while the pavement in front is flagged with tombstones. Inside, see the gilded and carved chapel of Senhor dos Passos and paintings of Saints Geronimus, Ambrose and Augustin.
Leave Largo da Igreja, with views south towards the Serra de Monte Figo, taking Rua Gago Coutinho to the Largo São Sebastião.

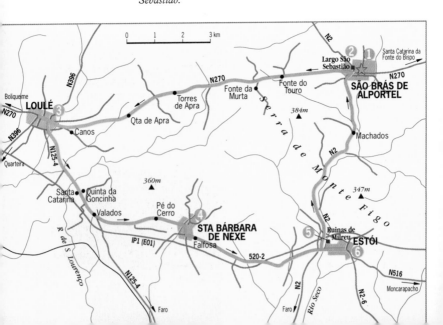

2 LARGO SÃO SEBASTIÃO

The bust in the small gardens in this
square is of Bernado Ramos, the
Portuguese poet and São Brás de
Alportel's most famous son.
_Turn left on to Rua Luís Bivar and
continue 13km to Loulé on the N270,
entering on the broad Avenida José da
Costa Mealha._

3 LOULÉ

The large Gothic parish church stands
on the Largo da Matriz, protected on
two sides by remains of the town's
Moorish walls. A smaller section of
fortifications near the Largo Dom Pedro
I has been incorporated into the
excellent small museum opposite the
Church of Nossa Senhora da Conceição
which, like the parish church, has good
decorative tiles (see pages 64–5).
_Leave Loulé via the Avenida Marçal
Pacheco (towards Faro). After 5km, at
Valados, take the turning for Santa
Bárbara de Nexe, just before the intersection
with the new motorway. Look back to the
right to see a very modern 'castle', recently
constructed as a private home._

4 SANTA BÁRBARA DE NEXE

The bell tower of the 15th-century
parish church rises above the roofs of the
village. Inside is a Manueline-style arch,
an early 18th-century tile panel depicting
St Barbara and a tiled sacristy.
_Take the Faro road and then turn left at
Falfosa on to the 520-2 to Estói. At the
crossroads with the N2 go straight on._

5 RUINAS DE MILREU

Before the village of Estói, the ruins of
Milreu (Tuesday to Sunday
10am–12:30pm, 2–5pm, admission free)
lie just off the road on the left. First
excavated in 1877, this Roman villa,

bath and temple complex was probably
connected to the nearby port of _Ossonoba_
(modern Faro). The remains include a
pagan temple later used as a Christian
church and bath mosaics depicting fish.
_Continue to Estói, parking near the parish
church of São Martinho, which is much
older than its 19th-century façade. At the
end of the street, to the left, a pair of
ornamental wrought-iron gates lead to one
of the Algarve's most astonishing sights, the
Palácio de Estói (free to grounds only)._

6 ESTÓI

The palace, a lavish rococo structure
built in the late 18th century, is closed
for restoration, but the gardens are very
fine. The path from the gates brings you
to a large marble fountain; go down the
steps to approach the palace. The many
statues depict Portuguese and foreign
luminaries, such as Castilho, Bocage,
Garrett, the Marquês de Pombal and
Milton. The tiled double staircase
conceals a grotto containing a replica of
Canova's _Three Graces_ and Roman
mosaics from Milreu.

Back at the large fountain and the
two smaller ones, look through the
coloured glass of the three doors behind
to see an ornate Christmas crib, whose
incredible detail can take a few seconds
to comprehend. The palace and its
chapel only become wholly visible from
the top staircase.
_Estói's market, on the second Sunday of the
month, is worth visiting. You can extend
this tour by following the Monte Figo hills
east, along the N516, to Moncarapacho, a
village with two churches of interest and
limestone caves (grutas) near by. Take the
N398 north and then the N270 west (near
another cave, the Gruta dos Arrifes) to
return to São Brás de Alportel. If not, take
the N2 from Estói direct to São Brás._

Estremoz

Arriving from the rolling plains at this, one of the Alentejo's most striking hilltowns, brings a true sense of discovery. Estremoz is an historic market town where time spent in thorough exploration will give you a real insight into the history and present day-life of this region (see pages 98–9). *Allow 2 hours.*

Start from the Rossio, the main square. You can park here any day except Saturday, when the town's famous market takes over. Cross to the smaller adjoining square to the north, dominated by a great expanse of water (or concrete, when the pond is empty).

1 LAGO DO GADANHA

The 17th-century Lago do Gadanha ('Scythe Lake') is named after the implement which Neptune waves, pennant-like above his head, in the middle of the pond. The church on the corner adjoining the Rossio is the Igreja de São Francisco (Church of St Francis) – originally part of a friary founded in the 13th century. Inside the Gothic church look for the tomb of Vasco Esteves Gato and a later Tree of Jesse.

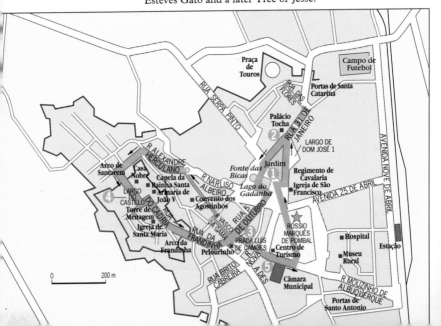

Leave the church and turn right into Largo de Dom José I, heading for the Palácio Tocha at the northern junction with Rua 31 de Janeiro.

2 PALÁCIO TOCHA

Step inside the entrance hall of the 17th-century palace with its a fine vaulted ceiling and *azulejo* tiles depicting the War of Independence against Spanish rule. Rua 31 de Janeiro and Rua das Flores lead to the bullring (Praça de Touros) and the ancient town gate, the Portas de Santa Catarina.

Return to the lake and, passing the Fonte das Bicas, a fountain in the shape of a pine cone, continue up Rua 5 de Outubro to the Praça Luís de Camões.

3 PRAÇA LUÍS DE CAMÕES

The fortifications of the upper town loom high above this square and its Manueline *pelourinho* (pillory).

If you have time, follow the signs which direct motorists from here, turning right and following Rua Vasco da Gama (the explorer was once a resident of Estremoz); this street runs below the regular white façade of the royal palace in the upper town. For a steeper, but shorter, route to the palace take the narrow pathway which branches left off Rua Vasco da Gama after a couple of minutes; the path climbs sharply to the left and rejoins the road as it enters the upper town through the Arco de Santarem, leading to the Largo do Castelo.

4 LARGO DO CASTELO

The elegant Largo do Castelo (Castle Square) is bordered by historic buildings and dominated by the grey Torre de Menagem. Part of this castle and palace complex has been converted into the Pousada da Rainha Santa Isabel, one of the best in the country. Within the castle

Grapes and pomegranates on sale in the market at Estremoz

is a chapel dedicated to Rainha Santa Isabel (Queen St Isabel, wife of King Dinis, both of whom lived in the castle in the 14th century). The chapel is decorated with beautiful *azulejos* depicting the life of Isabel. Alongside the castle is the 16th-century Igreja (Church) de Santa Maria.

Follow the ancient narrow street, Rua do Cadria, which leads away from the Igreja de Santa Maria, ending at the Arco da Frandinha. A sign directs you from here, down Rua da Frandinha, back to the Praça Luís de Camões. Cross this square to reach the Rossio with the vast façade of the Câmara Municipal (Town Hall) ahead.

5 CÂMARA MUNICIPAL

This 17th-century building was originally built as a convent dedicated to St Philip Neri, a former Bishop of Estremoz, and tiles depicting his life line the imposing staircase inside. On the eastern side of the Rossio is another former convent, the cloister of the Misericórdia and Cruzheiro, now a hospital. Next door is the Museu Rural, whose displays provide a comprehensive insight into the traditional ways of Alentejan life (open: 10am to 1pm and 3pm to 6pm, except Monday and holidays. Admission charge).

Évora

Capital of the Alentejo, Évora is one of the most elegant and historic cities in Portugal – a fact recognised by its UNESCO World Heritage Site status. This walking tour covers the principal monuments (see pages 102–5). *Allow 2 hours.*

Start at the Praça do Giraldo, at the geographical and commercial heart of the city, an elegant oblong bounded by balconied buildings and with a 16th-century fountain overlooked by the Renaissance São Antão church. Follow Rua de 5 de Outubro to the Largo Marquês de Marialva.

1 LARGO MARQUÊS DE MARIALVA

Here is Évora's great assembly of historic buildings: to the right the cathedral; ahead the former episcopal palace, now the Museu de Évora; to the left the Roman temple (Templo Romano) and the Convento dos Lóios, now one of the country's best-located *pousadas* (state-owned hotels). Further

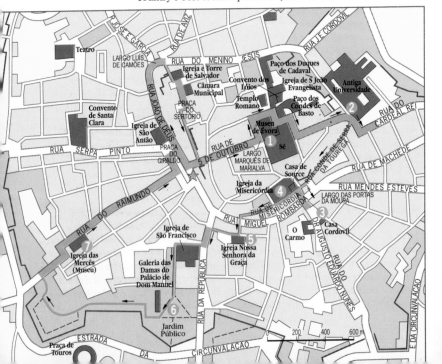

to the left the Paço dos Duques de Cadaval (the Palace of the Dukes of Cadaval) and its art gallery stands below the small formal park with its collection of statues, war memorial and good views from the terrace.

Return past the Roman temple and walk under an arch behind the cathedral apse, passing a Gothic building known as the Mansion of the Counts of Portalegre. Turn left and follow the street to the university.

2 ANTIGA UNIVERSIDADE

The 16th-century university has a two-tier cloister and the classrooms leading off are decorated with *azulejo* panels depicting the various subjects taught.

Follow Rua Conde de Serra da Tourega: half way along, on the right, note the house dated 1866, and covered with tiles. At the next square bear left into Largo das Portas da Moura.

3 LARGO DAS PORTAS DA MOURA

At the far end of this square is the Casa Cordovil, with its elegant Manueline and Moorish balcony, roughly contemporary with the square's globe-shaped fountain (the symbol of King Manuel I's growing empire). In the opposite direction, two towers from the original city walls stand in front of the house of the Renaissance scholar, Garcia de Resende.

Turn left at Resende's house, down Rua de Misericórdia, to the Misericórdia church.

4 IGREJA DA MISERICÓRDIA

This church is often closed: if it is open (before mass is a good time to try) the sacristan will be happy to show you the ornate tiled interior, the gilded altar and, upstairs, the vestments and small museum.

Continue through the small square, taking the second stepped passage down into the square to the left.

5 IGREJA NOSSA SENHORA DA GRAÇA

The façade of this small church has a flamboyant display of Renaissance sculpture topped with four giants.

Leave the square, taking Rua da República to Praça 1 de Maio, where the Church of São Francisco houses the macabre Capela dos Ossos (see page 103). Follow the road south to enter the Jardim Público (Public Gardens).

6 JARDIM PÚBLICO

To the right of the bandstand, paired Moorish windows line the so-called Galeria das Damas do Palácio de Dom Manuel. This is illuminated at night and stands near the remains of an earlier palace. The gardens follow part of the city's 17th-century fortifications; from the walls you can see the turreted 15th-century Ermida (Hermitage) de São Brás, where the sentences of the Inquisition were meted out and, to the right, the bullring (Praça de Touros).

Leave the park by the gate in Rua do Raimundo and turn right to reach the Igreja das Mercês.

7 IGREJA DAS MERCÊS

This church, built in 1669, has been transformed into the museum of decorative arts noted for its collection of *azulejos* (open: daily 10am to 12.30pm and 2pm to 5pm except Monday and holidays. Admission charge).

Continue up Rua do Raimundo to Praça do Giraldo. To see some of the best arcaded streets take Rua João de Deus to Largo Luís de Camões; return to Rua de 5 de Outubro via Igreja e Torre de Salvador, the Câmara Municipal and the Praça do Sertório.

Faro

Despite its off-putting suburbs, Faro at heart is a lively place whose old quarter has one of the most elegant squares in the Algarve. This walking tour is best done in the relative cool of the morning. *Allow 2 hours.*

Start from the Praça da Liberdade, the commercial centre of town, next to the main car-park. Turn left down Rua Dr João Lucio, passing a post office (Correio) *on the left, then turn right into Rua Mouzinho de Albuquerque.*

1 RUA MOUZINHO DE ALBUQUERQUE
The streets in this area are named after Portuguese writers and poets and the street signs, made of attractive tiles, give

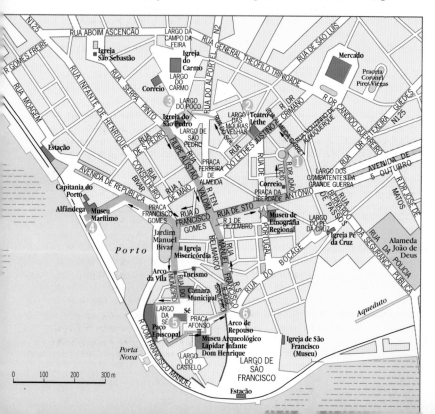

short biographical details of each. The area has some interesting buildings, including the astonishing Vivenda Mardlia, on the corner of Rua Almeida Garret, an ochre-coloured creation of fantastic decoration. At the end of the street, Alfarrabista is a bookshop in the old tradition.
Turn left down Rua Dr Justino Crimano to the small square dominated by the Ministry of Culture building, with its white façade and green windows.

2 TEATRO LETHE

Formerly the Jesuit college of Santiago Maior, today this building houses occasional exhibitions – and one of the Algarve's greatest treasures, the Teatro Lethe. During office hours, enquire from the concierge if you can see the *teatro, por favor,* and you should be escorted to the tiny ornate masterpiece – a reproduction in miniature of Milan's opera house, La Scala.
Cross Largo das Mouras Velhas and the gardens of Rua da Conceição. The bust you will see is of Portuguese writer Assis Esperanca. Turn right up Rua do Sol. Cross Rua do Alportel and the Largo do Poço to enter the imposing Largo do Carmo.

3 LARGO DO CARMO

To one side is the baroque Igreja do Carmo, the Carmelite Church, whose cemetery contains the macabre Capela dos Ossos (Chapel of Bones). Near by is the smaller Igreja do São Pedro.
Take Rua Filipe Alistão – looking out for the traditional grocer's store at No 26 – and cross the small square to reach the busy pedestrianised shopping streets which lead to the harbour. Turn right for Praça Francisco Gomes and the palm trees of the Jardim Manuel Bivar.

4 MUSEU MARÍTIMO

For the best view of the harbour, walk out to the Museu Marítimo (Maritime Museum). The harmonious frontage of the harbourside buildings, particularly the Igreja Misericórdia and the ornate Arco da Vila, is thanks to one of the city's most prominent citizens – Francisco Gomes de Avelar, Bishop of Faro in the late 18th century – under whose instructions much of the town was rebuilt after the earthquake of 1755.
Return to the Jardim Manuel Bivar and enter the old town by the Arco da Vila. By the Restaurant.

5 LARGO DA SÉ

Elegant Rua do Município climbs to the picturesque Largo da Sé, dominated by the cathedral (open weekends 10am–noon) and the Paço Episcopal (Bishop's Palace). Follow the narrow streets to the statue of Afonso III guarding the former convent of Nossa Senhora da Assunção, now the Museu Arqueológico (see page 60).
Leave the old town via the restored Arco de Repouso, where you can see a bronze casting of the city's Moorish charter. To the right is the vast Largo de São Francisco and its church. Turn left along Rua José Bandeiro.

6 RUA JOSÉ BANDEIRO

Beneath the walls a low plaque of *azulejos* depicts the *Tomada de Faro* – the reconquest of the city from the Moors by the Christians in 1249. On the corner behind stands another remarkably decorative building, this time in art nouveau style.
Continue along Rua Manuel Belmarco to join Rua de Santo António, the main shopping street, which leads back to Praça da Liberdade and the Museu de Etnografia Regional (closed weekends).

Ferragudo Beaches

Rumour has it that Ferragudo, a 16th-century fishing village facing Portimão across the Arade estuary, will soon be *the* place to live on the Algarve. The best view of the village is the approach from Portimão, with its cluster of white houses, topped by the church, reflected in the waters of the Arade river. Several of those houses are now being renovated; art galleries are opening and restaurants advertising 'Good Grub' stand next to those offering more traditional *cataplana* (fish casserole) and *arroz de marisco* (seafood with rice). Between Ferragudo and the hamlet of

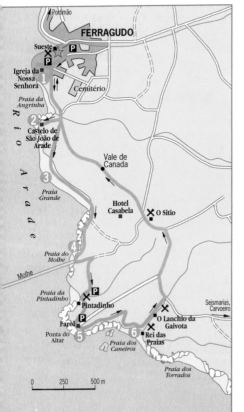

Seismarias, to the east, a series of red, green and blue arrows have been painted on walls along the roadside indicating three lengthy walks around the lanes and the coast. This walk follows part of the red route (in reverse) which includes the village of Ferragudo itself. You may prefer to drive, rather than walk, from the church in Ferragudo to the Praia Grande and on to the *molhe* (seawall) and the lighthouse; from there you can make a shorter, circular walk to the Praia dos Caneiros. If you do the whole route on foot, the total distance is about 9km. *Allow 2 hours.*

Start in Ferragudo, parking alongside the Igreja da Nossa Senhora on Largo Marcelino Franco.

1 IGREJA DA NOSSA SENHORA

The Igreja da Nossa Senhora is an attractive church with a statue of the *Virgin and Child* in a niche on the south wall. Opposite stands a monument in the shape of an anchor and a portrait of

Lord Baden-Powell, commemorating the foundation of Ferragudo's Sea Scout group, No 413.

From here you can walk, or drive, south following signs to the Praia Grande, passing the Cruzeiro da Senhora da Conceição where the road approaches the coast and the Praia da Angrinha beach near a junction of several roads. Take the lane to the right.

2 CASTELO DE SÃO JOÃO DE ARADE

The lane leads to the handsome Castelo de São João de Arade, overlooking the river from its headland. Built in the 17th century to guard the estuary – together with the Forte de Santa Catharina on the opposite bank – it has been a private residence since its restoration from ruins by the poet Coelho de Carvalho.

Return to the road junction and follow the first lane right to Praia Grande.

3 PRAIA GRANDE

As its name (Great Beach) suggests, this is indeed a long sweep of sand, whose waters are protected from the Atlantic waves by the *molhe* (seawall) to the south and which has become known in the Algarve as one of the best beaches for windsurfing. You can buy or hire equipment at the beach and there are several popular bars and restaurants. Walk north along the sand for another view of the castle.

Walk along the full length of the beach (the sand can be very soft) and scramble up the cliffs to walk along the clifftops to the molhe.

4 PRAIA DO MOLHE

This small beach lies on either side of the long *molhe* which juts out into the Arade estuary almost meeting another seawall coming from the Portimão side. You can walk out along the wall, a favourite place for fishermen.

Walk along the lane leading away from the beach and turn right to make the short descent to another sheltered sandy beach, the Praia da Pintadinho. This also has a beach restaurant and larger waves, being on the Atlantic, rather than the Arade. To avoid having to retrace your steps, it is possible to climb up to the cliffs near the lighthouse to reach the Ponta do Altar.

5 PONTA DO ALTAR

The Ponta do Altar is the southwestern-most point on the Ferragudo coast, guarded by an inhabited lighthouse, or *farol*. From the lighthouse there are views across the *molhe* to Portimão. You can walk east along the clifftop – again meeting the occasional red arrow, pointing in the opposite direction to the way you are going – with views to the beaches below. Look out among the low gorse bushes for the tiny snails *(caramujos)* which are a local delicacy.

The path crosses a valley, past a new villa development, before joining the lane that leads down to the Praia dos Caneiros.

6 PRAIA DOS CANEIROS

You will pass a small restaurant in the lane and there is another on the beach itself. The sand is backed by the usual golden sandstone cliffs with low arches beginning to be eroded at their base. At low tide you can walk around the small western headland to another bay, the Praia dos Torrados.

From the Praia dos Caneiros it is a 3.5km walk back to Ferragudo along the lane, continuing straight over at the crossroads which leads left to the molhe and right to O Sitio restaurant.

Castles and Caves around Loulé

This 62km tour takes in some of the Algarve's more ancient landmarks – both natural (the waterfall at Alte and the caves of Rocha da Pena and Rocha dos Soidos) and man-made (the Moorish castles of Salir and Paderne). *Allow 4 hours.*

From Loulé take the Salir road through Assumada. After 7km you will cross the Algibre river at the Roman bridge – the Ponte de Tor. Here you can detour right to follow the Fonte de Benémola walk (see page 40). Otherwise, continue on to Salir and cross the Ribeira (River) dos Moinhos, to park near the church.

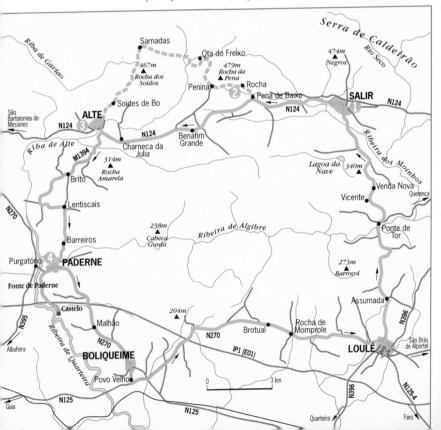

1 SALIR

If the church is open, look inside to see the illuminated 1550 Papal Bull signed by Pope Paul III. Until the reconquest by Alphonso III in 1248, Salir was a Moorish stronghold with a mighty castle. As early as the 16th century the fortress was in ruins and the present village was built over the Muslim settlement. The remaining walls stand to the west of the church; follow the road up past the café on the left, with views of the village to the right. Much of the walls were built of _taipa,_ a mixture of clay, sand, straw and water, typical of the Almóada period of Moorish architecture. Excavations have revealed a kitchen area and cooking pots. There is a market on the last Sunday of the month.
From Salir follow the N124 west towards Alte. After 4km turn right at Pena de Baixo and continue for 1km to Rocha.

2 ROCHA

The Rocha da Pena, at 479m, is an ancient outcrop of the Serra do Caldeirão mountain range, which lies to the northwest and has remains of Moorish, Roman and even neolithic occupation. From the village of Rocha, a footpath leads round the lower slopes of the outcrop, returning alongside a group of windmills. If you wish, you can drive east of Alte to the Rocha dos Soidos, or explore on foot. Both hills have deep caves, or _grutas._
If you do not follow the diversion, return to the N124 and continue west to Alte via Benafim, which has a monthly market every first Saturday and an annual fair in late October.

3 ALTE

Alte is regarded as the prettiest of the Algarve villages and there is plenty to detain you here. You can explore the nearby _fontes_ or springs, the tiled, vaulted parish church, the São Luís chapel and the Queda do Vigario waterfall – as well as several cafés and restaurants (see page 51). The Fonte Grande is backdrop both to the May Day Festival and to the Folklore Festival on the second Sunday in August.
Leave Alte by the N124 Salir road, then turn right on to the M1394 to Paderne via Brito and Lentiscais.

4 PADERNE

Paderne is another ancient village with a Moorish heritage, although its ruined castle, recaptured from the Moors in 1248, stands some distance away, to the south of the Via Infante motorway. Follow the road to Fonte de Paderne, southwest of the village, passing the spring itself on your right, and continue along a track with the castle ahead. Inside the castle see the ruined Gothic chapel. Below the castle a steep path leads down into the valley and across to the opposite hill via an ancient and remote Roman bridge. In Paderne itself, see the 16th-century parish church, which was rebuilt after the 1755 earthquake, the Nossa Senhora do Pé chapel and the remains of the Gothic fortifications. The village celebrates several feasts and festivals in Holy Week and throughout the summer, including the annual fair of São Tiago (25 July) and the Pé da Cruz feast (mid-October).
If you collect unusual place-names, you may like to make a 1km detour west of Paderne to the hamlet of Purgatório. Otherwise, head south to Boliqueime on the N270, where there is a concentration of restaurants specialising in piri-piri _(spicy chicken) and a market on the last Thursday of the month, then east to Loulé on the N270._

Around Portimão

Portimão lies between the estuaries of two major rivers, the Alvor and the Arade, an area with fascinating evidence of earlier inhabitants – a Roman villa at Abicada and a neolithic burial chamber at Alcalar. A visit to the Museu Regional in Lagos is essential to help interpret the sites. You can combine this tour with the Ferragudo walk (page 32). *Allow 4 hours.*

From Portimão town centre take the new dual carriageway south to Praia da Rocha and then follow the coast road past a series of beaches and resorts to Alvor.

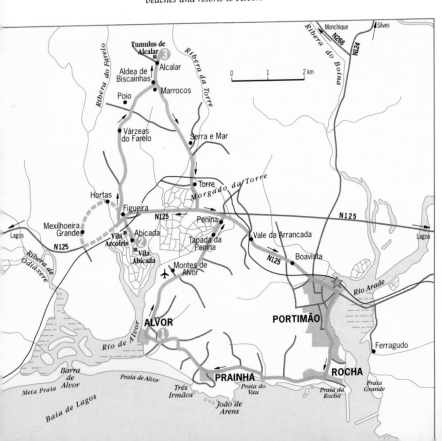

1 ALVOR

This fishing village on the Alvor estuary is historic rather than pretty (see page 51), but it has a good selection of restaurants. Worth visiting is the fish market (*lota*) and the interesting parish church which overlooks the harbour. At low tide you can see villagers wading on to the sandbanks – the habitat of black-winged stilts, terns and other wetland birds – to collect shellfish.

From Alvor head back towards the N125 northwards, passing a small airport, a modern church and a casino. At the next junction, turn left, passing the Penina Hotel and golf-course, turning left again after 4km at the crossroads opposite Figueira. Bear right at the fork and then left up a narrow cobbled track by the Vila Arcolris. Cross the railway line and follow a line of cypress trees which lead past the base of a ruined fort overgrown with trees.

The Tumulus de Alcalar

2 VILA ABICADA

The road ends at a group of white farm buildings to the side of which lie the remains of the Roman Vila Abicada, with substantial areas of mosaic intact. Although the regional council has announced plans to restore this, and the neolithic site at Alcalar, work is governed by availability of funds; in this case you will be faced with a brief explanatory sign which is actually upside-down when you come to interpret it. The villa dates from the 4th century, and most of the excavated finds are now in the Museu Regional in Lagos.

Retrace your route to the N125. If you wish to detour through the quaint village of Mexilhoeira Grande, turn left on to the N125, then right. Mexilhoeira Grande has an interesting parish church with two side doors decorated with 16th-century Manueline carvings. If you do not take this detour, cross the N125 and drive through the village of Figueira, continuing north through a valley of orchards, and turning right at the junction to Poio. Pass through this hamlet and turn left at the next junction opposite a blue house. After less than 1km turn right, down a track signed to the 'Gourmet Restaurant'.

3 TUMULUS DE ALCALAR

After less than 20m, on the left, look for a place to park and take the path that leads from the track between two barbed wire fences. At the top is the Tumulus de Alcalar – as yet unrestored – which resembles an elaborate flint-walled well with a large stone slab and a channel down the slope to the right. It is a megalithic grave of the tholoi type – that is, a chamber and corridor – and dates from the period 2000–600 BC. A 19th-century engraving of a cross-section of the tomb, together with relics found during its excavation, can be seen in the Museu Regional in Lagos.

Return to the road but continue straight ahead for Torre, at the first junction, passing a wayside crucifix on the right and an agricultural aqueduct. Drive under a narrow railway bridge and, after less than 1km, rejoin the N125 almost opposite Penina. Turn left to return to Portimão.

Prehistoric Alentejo

This circular motor tour of 75km takes in five prehistoric sites west of Évora, including a stone circle, the largest dolmen on the Iberian peninsula and cave paintings deep underground. Some of the roads are unmetalled and may be difficult after heavy rain. *Allow 4 hours.*

From Évora, take the E90/N114 towards Montemor-o-Novo. After 10km, leave the main road to turn left at the sign to Guadalupe.

1 GUADALUPE

The small chapel on the right before the hamlet is the Capela de Guadalupe, founded in 1609. It was destroyed during a cyclone in 1941 but has since been restored.
Drive through Guadalupe to the junction at the far side: go straight across, following the sign to the Cromleque dos Almendres.

2 CROMLEQUE DOS ALMENDRES

Follow the signs to drive through a fertile valley, past a Cooperativa Agrícola (Agricultural Co-operative). The road passes through an olive grove and ends abruptly at a picnic

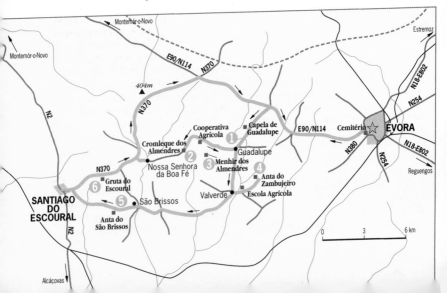

table. On the left is the cromlech –
a circle of some 95 stones, arranged in
an oval on a gentle slope and known
locally as Pedras Talhas, 'the Hewn
Stones'.

*Return through the olive grove to the Co-
operative and park on the grass verge. Walk
in front of the farmhouse towards the grain
silos, following a blue arrow painted on the
wall. Bear right at a broken wall heading
towards an olive grove where the next
menhir stands between two rows of trees.*

3 MENHIR DOS ALMENDRES

The granite menhir stands 2.5m tall,
broader on two of its sides so that it is
oval, rather than circular, in plan – a
remarkable intrusion into a peaceful
landscape where your only companions
are likely to be lapwings, and cattle
wearing leather straps around their
necks, some with bells, traditionally
made in the nearby village of Alcáçovas.
*Return to the junction at Guadalupe and
turn right to Valverde, passing the village
wash-house and a sandy football pitch,
driving along a ridged, compacted sand
road. Cross a stream and drive through
young eucalyptus trees growing on land that
belongs to the Évora University agricultural
station, whose buildings appear on the
horizon before the village of Valverde. At
the junction with a metalled road, opposite a
café, turn left. Cross over the marshy river,
passing a water tower, and turn left at the
sign to Anta do Zambujeiro, passing
through the yard of the agricultural station.
Take the left-hand gate, recrossing the
stream, and branch left again, following a
sign for parking.*

4 ANTA DO ZAMBUJEIRO

Leave your car here and cross the stream
via the planks, heading towards the
corrugated iron shelter which has been

built around this massive dolmen amid a
cacophony of clattering cowbells. The
excavated finds from the site can be seen
in the Museu de Évora in Évora.
*Return through Valverde, continuing past
the football pitch and a modern church with
a large blue cross, into scarred countryside,
which then gives way to vines and
eucalyptus.*

5 ANTA DO SÃO BRISSOS

Beyond the Ermida (Hermitage) of
Nossa Senhora de Livramenta Anta, and
the turning to the village of São Brissos,
another dolmen has been incorporated
into the tiny chapel of São Brissos, lying
off the road to the right.
*After another 5km the road joins the N370.
Turn right, away from the village of
Santiago do Escoural, for the last prehistoric
site – the underground paintings at the
Gruta do Escoural, just over 1km from the
junction, on the right.*

6 GRUTA DO ESCOURAL

There is off-road parking in front of the
high metal fence, whose gate will be
locked if the custodian is not available to
show you the paintings. The experience
is not for the faint-hearted; from a small
opening in the hillside a ladder descends
into blackness which is only lit by the
guide's flickering paraffin lamp. You
eventually reach a large chamber,
inhabited by bats, and the guide traces
the outline of horses on the walls,
explaining to non-Portuguese speakers
that these were the food of the neolithic
artist. There is no charge for the visit,
but the guide will appreciate a tip – a
small price to pay for the relief of being
back above ground.
*On the return trip to Évora, via the N370
and E90, you can detour to visit the church
at Nossa Senhora da Boa Fé.*

A Walk to the Fonte de Benémola

The hills north of Loulé are a world away from the villas of 'tourist Algarve'; they are riddled with caves and springs and ancient villages lie in the valleys between. Querença and its sister village, Aldeia da Tor, date back to Roman times and are separated by the fertile valley of the Ribeira da Fonte Menalva. You can follow the valley upstream to the Fonte de Benémola, a spring which joins the river at a shallow fording point classified as an area of natural interest, and then return along the opposite bank. The circuit is 4km but you can extend it further into the valley and explore the villages themselves, or incorporate the walk into the motor tour from Loulé (see page 34). *Allow 3 hours.*

Follow the N396 10km north of Loulé then turn left on to the N524 passing the turning to Querença. The start of the path to the Fonte de Benémola is signposted 3km after the turning, to the right just before a left-hand bend. If you pass the Quinta da Passagem and bridge over the river you have gone too far. Park on the grass verge just at the bottom of the sandy track.

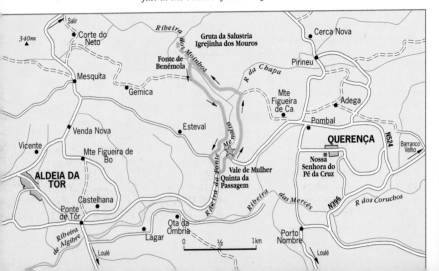

The walk starts in an area known as the Vale de Mulher, where a group of houses lies between the stream and the track. The fertile floodplain along the banks is divided into cultivated smallholdings where solitary farmers tend vegetables, fruit and almond trees. Water is brought to the fields by water-wheels (a *nora* in Portuguese) located at the side of the stream.

After walking for just over 1km you will pass a path that branches off to the right to another group of cottages. Keep on the main track which bears left and crosses a tributary of the main stream, the Ribeira da Chapa.

The path returns towards the main stream again (ignore another path off to the right) and soon follows alongside the water. After less than 1km you will arrive at the *fonte* (spring) – here the stream opens out and is crossed by a rocky ford, passable with care but beware of mossy stones; there is a picnic table next to the stone piers built out into the water. The path continues to follow the stream bed (all but dry above here) into the valley, but a section of large boulders makes the going quite difficult at first. The ravine narrows and can be eerily silent: in the hillside above and to the right are two local caves of repute – the cavernous Gruta da Salustria and the Igrejinha dos Mouros ('the Church of the Moors') both of which have stalactites and stalagmites.

Return to the ford and cross to the right bank.

The shady path follows closer to the water on this side, past more small springs (*nascentes*); in its lower sections the land is again cultivated. In spring look out for arum lilies growing alongside the path.

NEARBY VILLAGES

The nearby villages are also worth exploring, especially Querença. The Church of Nossa Senhora do Pé da Cruz has a Manueline doorway and, if you find it open, *azulejos* inside. The church at Aldeia da Tor is dedicated to Santa Rita, and the bridge which crosses the Algibre river, to the hamlet of Ponte de Tor, is Roman.

Even better would be to visit the villages during one of their annual fairs. Aldeia da Tor has a wine festival on 16 January while Querença's Festa das Chouriças – celebrating the local smoked sausage – also takes place in late January. There are more festivities at Easter, on 24 June for the festival of São João (St John), and again on 15 August, the Feast of Nossa Senhora da Assunção.

Ignore the paths to the right and, after nearly 2km, you will pass a group of cork oaks before dropping down to rejoin the road next to the bridge. Turn left and walk a short way back along the N524 to your car.

The rocky ford at the junction of the Fonte de Benémola and the main stream

EXPATS AND FOREIGNERS

Portugal's 'special relationship' with Britain goes back over 600 years making it the longest-lasting alliance in Europe. England provided the Portuguese with a queen when John of Gaunt's daughter, Philippa of Lancaster, married King João I in 1387. The compliment was returned when, in 1662, King Charles II of England married Catherine of Bragança, the daughter of King João IV. On the commercial front the port wine trade is very much a joint Anglo-Portuguese venture and a strong British presence has existed in Oporto, the centre of the industry, for the last 300 years.

More recently, the Algarve has acted as something of a magnet for British people who, lured by the temperate climate, have chosen to live there. On the one hand there are those who have capitalised on the tourist boom, opening up hotels, bars and discothèques, and on the other there are the more elderly people who see it as the perfect place to retire. Several of the major resorts have areas where English bars and cafés seem to outnumber native ones.

By contrast, though a sizeable number of non-Portuguese live in the Alentejo, few of them are British. After the apparent failure of the co-operatives to manage the newly nationalised large farms (following the 1974 Carnation Revolution) much of the land was either returned to its original owners or sold off. This proved an attractive proposal to a number of Danes and Germans who took over all or part of some properties. There is also a German air base in the Alentejo and the Alentejan coast seems to be particularly popular with young and footloose German travellers.

Many expatriates find the climate, accommodation and facilities on offer in Portugal an attractive proposition

The Algarve

*T*he Algarve coastline stretches for over 150km, from the Rio (River) Guadiana, on the Spanish frontier in the east, to the windswept Punta de Sagres peninsula in the west. Given the sheer number of beaches, from tiny coves to seemingly infinite ribbons of sand, it is small wonder that over half of all visitors to Portugal choose to concentrate on this southern strip.

Geographically surrounded by the Atlantic Ocean, the province is nevertheless Mediterranean in mood. The sun shines for over 3,000 hours a year, the hillsides are dotted with olive and almond trees and the lifestyle is leisurely. Only the high tides and the cool sea temperatures will remind you that this is not the Mediterranean.

East of Faro the flat coast of salt-pans, sandbars and islets attracts more migratory birds than tourists. The majority of the holiday resorts lie to the west, between Faro and Lagos, situated along a stunning coastline of cliffs, curiously shaped rocks and grottoes. Some of the resorts have developed around pretty fishing villages, while others are positive eyesores dumped on the sides and tops of the cliffs. Yet even giant developments like Albufeira manage to retain some of their former charm. Fishing communities still thrive, supplying the sardines which sizzle on back-street braziers all along the coast. This is especially true west of Lagos, where the rising cliffs culminate at Sagres, with its awesome fortress and angry seas.

Coastal Algarve lies to the south of the main national highway, the N125. North of this road, the spirit of the old Algarve survives and you don't have to drive far inland to find sleepy whitewashed villages where locals nod over a glass of wine or liqueur and storks nest in the church belfries.

Driving is the simplest way of getting to know the region but be prepared for manic drivers and pot-holes, as well as horsedrawn carts, and herds of goats – all of which, of course, are part of the charm of the unexplored Algarve.

ALBUFEIRA

From a quaint fishing village Albufeira has grown into a giant cosmopolitan resort. Even so, there is far more to Albufeira than first meets the eye. Clinging to the cliffs above the main beach lies the old town, with its distinctive Moorish flavour. The narrow cobbled alleys, lined by whitewashed cottages, lead down to terraces overlooking the sea and the beach. Further proof that all is not destroyed is the Praia dos Barcos or Fishermen's Beach, where brightly painted fishing boats are drawn up on the sands. At night you can see the lights of the sardine boats out at sea and early in the morning you can watch the catch being auctioned at the old fish market.

Albufeira's monuments are limited to a handful of churches, including the pretty 16th-century Chapel of the Misericórdia in the old town and the Church of São Sebastião, whose portal is carved with swirling Manueline motifs.

The main beach lies below the town; access is through a tunnel under the Sol e Mar Hotel or down the cliffside steps. (These, and the steep cobbled streets, make access for disabled visitors difficult.) The sea here is safe for children. The main drawback is crowding. Less crowded are São Rafael, 5km west, Praia da Rocha (see page 74) or Olhos de Agua, 7km east.

Location: Albufeira is 39km west of Faro and 52km east of Lagos. Tourist office: Rua 5 de Outubro. Tel: 089 512144. Open: daily 9.30am–12.30pm, 2–5.30pm; 9.30am–7pm in summer.

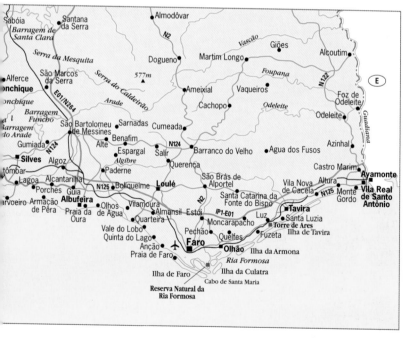

ALCOUTIM

Only the placid waters of the Rio (River) Guadiana divide Alcoutim from its former Spanish rival, Sanlúcar de Guadiana. So close are these riverside villages that you can sometimes spot the storks nesting in the Spanish belfries on the other bank.

Originally a fortified stronghold and strategic river port, Alcoutim has, in recent centuries, been no more than a sleepy waterside village, with fishing and handicrafts as its main activities. Far removed from the frenzy of the coast, it still attracts only a sprinkling of visitors. To most tourists, and even to some of the expatriates who live at the other end of the province, Alcoutim is, or has been up to now, no more than a dot on the map. Now, however, with the opening of the bridge astride the Guadiana, linking Spain to southern Portugal, and the completion of a 52-bed hotel in Alcoutim itself, the resort is likely to see many more visitors in the near future.

Another draw will be the 212-hectare wildlife reserve and safari resort, still in its embryonic stage, being laid out in the mountains west of Alcoutim.

Above the centre of Alcoutim a ruined castle stands on a hillock; from here you have a bird's-eye view of Portuguese and Spanish fishing smacks, swish foreign yachts and frontier guards spying out the land for smugglers. The

Eating out beneath the snow-white walls of Alcoutim, on the Spanish border

other sights of Alcoutim are the parish Church, by the river, with a Renaissance portal and the Church of Nossa Senhora da Conceição at the top of the village with a Manueline portal and 18th-century altarpiece.

The loveliest drive in this region follows the banks of the Guadiana for about 19km downstream to Foz de Odeleite, joining the main N122 between Odeleite and Azinhal. From the river bank you glimpse the quiet hills of southern Spain, while on the Portuguese side lies the occasional riverside hamlet where locals till the lush land or tend to small patches of vines and vegetables.

To see the handicrafts of the region call at the tiny tourist office in the centre of Alcoutim which will provide you with a leaflet detailing the specialist crafts of the regional villages; these include pottery, basketry, blankets and rugs made to centuries-old designs.

Handicrafts aside, a drive through the rolling hills west of Alcoutim, and a detour to one or two of the isolated villages, will give you a real taste of one of the most remote regions of the Algarve.

Location: Alcoutim is on the N122, 44km north of Vila Real de Santo António. Tourist office: open daily 9.30am–8pm in summer; and 9.30am–5.30pm October to April. Tel: 081 46179.

ALJEZUR

Lying between the sea and the mountains of western Algarve, Aljezur is a small town spread below the ruins of its Moorish fortress. The remains, reached via steep streets through the somewhat shabby Moorish quarter, provide a fine panorama of the surrounding countryside.

Bridge over the Aljezur river

The muddy Aljezur river, reduced to a mere trickle in summer, divides the old quarter from the featureless 'new' town. This was built in 1795 when the mosquito-infected old quarter was declared a hazard zone.

Proximity to peaceful beaches is one of the town's main attractions. To the northwest, Amoreira and Monte Clérigo lie either side of a silted-up estuary and both have large expanses of empty sands. At Arrifana, 10km southwest of Aljezur, a big beach makes up for the drab village set on the cliffs above.

Some 17km north of Aljezur, the remote but picturesque little village of Odeceixe marks the last stop before the Algarve gives way to the Alentejo. The wide river valley, dotted with camper-vans, leads to a peaceful, sheltered beach.

Location: Aljezur is on the N120, 30km northwest of Lagos.

AZULEJOS

The *azulejo,* or glazed tile, is one of the most characteristic features of Portuguese decorative art. At one time only wealthy Portuguese could afford to live in a house decorated with tiles. Nowadays the *azulejo* is completely classless, decorating the façades of even the simplest dwellings.

It was the Moorish influence that led to the Portuguese passion for *azulejos.* Nobody agrees about the origin of the word, but it may be derived from the Arabic *al Zulaicha* or *Zuleija,* meaning ceramic mosaic, or simply from the Portuguese word *azul,* meaning blue.

Tiles really came into vogue during the period from 1580 to 1640 when Portugal was under Spanish rule. The earliest tiles were imported from Andalucia, but soon the

Bar sign in Monchique

RUA DO Dr. PEREIRA DE SOUSA NOTAVEL GEÓLOGO e GRANDE AMIGO DO ALGARVE 1870–1931

BAR Travessa

Commemorative street sign in Faro

Portuguese started to develop their own. The second half of the 17th century saw the arrival of the narrative tiles. Churches were subsequently decorated with biblical scenes, and private palaces with fables, hunting scenes or depictions of everyday life. By the middle of the 18th century tiled scenes had become lavish and were typified by floral designs, cherubs and hedonistic scenes, influenced by rococo painters. However, the rebuilding of Portugal after the catastrophic earthquake of 1755 led to the mass production of *azulejos* in simpler styles. Fortunately, some of the small family businesses, using traditional tilemaking techniques, managed to survive.

In the Algarve the Church of São Lourenço, Almansil (see page 50), stands out for its gloriously tiled interior. Also worth seeing are the antique tiled panels in the gardens at Estói (see page 25) and the tiled scenes from the life of St Francis in the Church of São Francisco in Faro (see page 59).

In the Alentejo the finest examples can be found in the cloister and chapter house of the Convent of Nossa Senhora da Conceição in Beja (see page 96) and in the church of the Convento dos Lóios in Évora (see page 102).

A comtemporary portrait of
St Francis

Eighteenth-century tiles in São
Lourenço church, Almansil

ALMANSIL

Patterned chimneys and pottery are the
main features of the small unassuming
town of Almansil. But, lying by the
frenzied N125 highway, it is not a place
to linger long.

São Lourenço

What most tourists come to see is the
stunningly beautiful little church in
the nearby village of São Lourenço.
Sitting on a hillock east of Almansil, the
church and its splendid tiled interior
provide an oasis of peace and a feast for
the eyes.

Apart from the sumptuous gilded
altar, the entire church, including the
vaulted ceiling, is embellished with blue
and white glazed tiles – or *azulejos* –

showing the life of St Lawrence.

The tiles are dated 1730 and signed
by Policarpo de Oliveira Bernardes who,
together with his more famous father,
António, established a large workshop
and produced tiles which can be found
throughout Portugal. In true Algarvian
style there is no information available at
the church and the old ladies who sit
outside, hoping to collect your spare
escudos, can only converse in the local
dialect.

Also worth a visit is the local Centro
Cultural, below the church. This stylish
art gallery exhibits works by Portuguese
and foreign artists.
Church of São Lourenço, 2km east of

São Lourenço church

Almansil, off the N125. Open: daily, 9am–1pm, 2.30–6pm, but if closed the key is available from the house next door. Admission free.

Quinta do Lago

Just 6km south of Almansil is the Quinta do Lago complex where, from dawn to dusk 1,500 sprinklers keep the Algarve's most famous golf-course looking lush. The up-market complex covers 640 hectares, with luxury villas dotted among pinewoods and lakes. The Praia do Anção is a superb, and surprisingly uncrowded, beach.

Location: Almansil is on the N125, 13km northwest of Faro and 7km south of Loulé.

ALTE

It is not surprising that numerous excursion coaches choose to stop at Alte on their inland tours. Perhaps a little too pristine to be typical of inland Algarve, it is a pretty village of streams and waterfalls, cobbled streets with freshly whitewashed houses, delicate laced chimneys and balconies brimming with flowers. The village has long been known for the purity of its springs, and for centuries people have been coming here to take the fountain waters. Nowadays the banks of the stream make popular picnic spots and, during the summer months, folklore evenings are held at the Fonte Pequena (Little Fountain Inn).

The finest features of Alte's parish church are the finely carved Manueline portico and – if you can get inside – the 18th-century *azulejos* and colourful religious statuary. The quaint baroque chapel of São Luis stands on a small square at the other end of the village. The adjoining museum has a heterogeneous collection of cow bells,

Lifeboat station and fishing boat on the quayside at Alvor

rat traps, old pots and photographs of the Alte town band in the 1930s.
Location: Alte is on the N124, 11km east of São Bartolomeu de Messines.

ALVOR

Lying between Lagos and Portimão, Alvor consists of a picturesque hilltop fishing village and, well over 1km away, a huge stretch of exposed beach dominated by dreary tower blocks. In the village the tightly packed houses jostle around the parish church and slope down to the estuary quayside where the fishermen gather.

For a bird's-eye view of the whole area, take one of the sightseeing flights by aeroplane from Montes de Alvor, 2km north of the village.
Location: Alvor is 8km west of Portimão and 18km east of Lagos.

ARMAÇÃO DE PÊRA

Though the fishermen still haul their skiffs down the sands, Armaçâo de Pêra looks a far cry from the fishing village it used to be. The huge development spreads along the coastline, its high-rise blocks overlooking what the resort itself claims is the biggest beach in the Algarve; true or not, it certainly is vast.

To the east the wide band of golden sand is seemingly endless; to the west the beach gives way to curious rock formations with grottoes and small sandy coves, only accessible by fishing boat. One of the prettiest of the caves is Senhora da Rocha, about 2km west of Armaçâo de Pêra, which takes its name from the little Romanesque chapel perched on a rocky promontory above the glorious beach.

The new and ever-expanding development in Armacâo de Pêra has not entirely swallowed up the original village. In the centre, on the waterfront, are the ruins of an 18th-century fort

Armação, the Algarve's biggest beach

with a small chapel, dedicated to St Anthony. Vestiges of the old fishing quarter survive and you can still enjoy freshly caught fish and seafood in the cafés and restaurants.

Zoo Marine

Zoo Marine, to the northeast, is more of a mini funfair with a big wheel, merry-go-round and bouncy castles. Star attractions are the dolphins, the seals and the parrots who ride bicycles on a tight rope.
On the N125 between Guia and Alcantarilha. The zoo operates a pick-up service from various points between Portimão and Quarteira. Tel: 082 561104. Open: daily 10am–6pm, high season 10am–8pm. Admission charge.

Location: Armacâo de Pêra is 3km south of the N125 and about 47km west of Faro. Tourist office: Avenida Marginal. Tel: 082

312145. Open: daily 9.30am–12.30pm, 2–5.30pm; 9.30am–5.30pm weekends.

BURGAU

The small resort of Burgau lies at the sleepy west end of the Algarve – sleepy, that is, until the old road leading to this end of the Algarve was rebuilt as a modern highway, destroying some of the natural beauty of the region in the process.

Although Burgau has doubled in size over the last decade, with an increasing number of mini-markets and tourist shops, it still manages to preserve much of its charm as a fishing village. Fishermen mending nets or painting boats provide plenty of local colour, and tourists and locals seem to mix well, either in the British-run pubs or in the fishermens' cafés, where fresh sardines are still grilled on tiny charcoal burners.

Well south of the new main road, the centre of Burgau, consisting of red-roofed cottages and cobbled streets, is set on steep slopes above the beach, while the newer development and the discos are kept at arm's length. Normally Burgau has an all-sand beach but in recent years the early summer tides have washed the sands away, exposing the rocks. As an alternative, try the lovely Cabanes Velhal beach west of Burgau. There is also the swimming-pool, available to visitors staying in Burgau. The centre of the resort is sprinkled with restaurants where the standard is generally good. For a pleasant setting and reasonably priced Portuguese fare, try the beach bar.

Just outside the village is the British-run Burgau Sports Centre, offering excellent facilities for tennis, squash, volleyball and five-a-side football. Buy a drink or two and you are welcome to use the pool free of charge. Once a week the club organises a barbecue and folk night, with dancers from nearby Budens. *Location: Burgau is 18km west of Lagos.*

Whitewashed houses, terracotta tiles and cobbled streets in Burgau

FISHING

The Phoenicians are given the credit for first noting the annual migration of the tunny, or tuna fish, from the open waters of the Atlantic to the inshore waters of the Algarvian coast. Until quite recently the fish were caught in large traps, harpooned and then dragged on deck. The struggles between man and fish, which can grow as large as 450 kilos, were so bloody that they were dubbed 'bullfights of the sea'. Today the tunny population is much diminished and the catch, using modern methods such as sonar to locate the fish, takes place far out to sea.

Less spectacular, but no less important, are the shoals of sardine to be found in the deep waters off Cabo de São Vicente (Cape St Vincent) and off the coast of northwest Africa. A common sight, accompanied by an irresistible smell, is the grilling of freshly caught sardines over back-street charcoal braziers. When cooked, the fish is simply wrapped in bread and eaten in the street.

Portuguese fleets were fishing for cod off the coast of England as early as the 14th century. By the next century they had reached as far afield as Newfoundland, where they still fish today. Salted cod *(bacalhau)* is the national dish and it is said that there are as many recipes for preparing it as there are days in the year.

One of the victims of the modernisation of the fishing industry has been the Algarvian fishing dog. This looks like a rather scruffy poodle but its webbed paws and its love of the water made it a great boon to the fishermen. The dogs were trained to guide fish into nets, bark in the fog and swim from boat to boat with messages. They were also reputed to have saved many men from drowning. Today these dogs are quite rare but a programme has been devised to try and save the breed.

Fishing in the Algarve is still a
small-scale industry that lends
colour to the harbour areas and
the appetising smell of grilled
sardines to the streets

Tumbling rocks lead down to a glittering sea at Carvoeiro

CARVOEIRO

Carvoeiro is one of a string of overgrown fishing villages whose hills and headlands are now splashed with blindingly white villa constructions. Happily, though, the new development is restricted to the outskirts, leaving a centre which has a certain amount of colour and charm. Down by the beach the fishermen earn their living by taking tourists to the grottoes by day and fishing for sardines by night.

The beach, backed by ochre-coloured cliffs, is barely big enough to cope with the huge number of visitors that Carvoeiro now receives. The real beauty of this stretch of predominantly rocky coastline lies in its fascinating grottoes and secluded sandy coves. To the east of the resort lie the peaceful beaches of Marinha and Benagil (see page 22), but the top attraction of the area lies just 1km east of the centre, at Algar Seco.

Here a long flight of steps takes you down to a beauty spot where the pitted ochre cliffs have been eroded to form dramatic stone arches and grottoes. Provided that the waves are not crashing against the cliffs, the waters – deep blue and transparent – provide a paradise for snorkellers. The taverna on the rocks makes a lovely spot for a snack or a sundowner.

Lying roughly halfway between Lagos and Albufeira, Carvoeiro makes a good base for exploring the western half of the Algarve. Silves, Portimão and Lagos are all within easy reach and Monchique, in the mountains, makes a memorable excursion. For those who want to stay put, the centre of Carvoeiro is liberally endowed with cafés, bars, pubs and restaurants. The resort has two tennis-courts, squash-courts and a golf-course. *Location: Carvoeiro is 5km south of the N125, 13km east of Portimão. Tourist office: Largo da Praia. Tel: 082 357728. Open: daily 9.30am–8pm (winter 9.30am–5.30pm Monday to Friday; closed: weekends).*

CASTRO MARIM

Rising from the marshlands west of the Rio (River) Guadiana, the hilltown of Castro Marim enjoys a bird's-eye view of southern Spain. The town and its castle occupy a strategic position, protecting the southern Portuguese coast. The Phoenicians based themselves here while mining for copper and tin; the Moors then settled for several centuries until the Christians ejected them in 1242.

In 1319, the town became the headquarters of the Knights of Christ. This newly formed military order played an instrumental role in the early voyages that marked the beginning of the Great Age of Discovery. Prince Henry the Navigator was appointed governor of the order and, if the inscription inside the castle entrance is to be believed, he was once a resident here.

Set within massive walls, the main hilltop castle of Castro Marim dominates the town and was built by King Afonso III in the 13th century. It was laid ruin by the 1755 earthquake but the battlemented walls and a ruined church still survive.

Take a tour from the battlements, which provide a splendid panorama over the surrounding countryside. The

The hilltown of Castro Marim

Castro Marim's main church

fortress of São Sebastião, built four centuries after the castle, can be seen sitting on a hillock to the southwest. To the east lies the Spanish border town of Ayamonte, while to the south is the Portuguese border town of Vila Real de Santo António.

Spread out below are the flat salt-pans of the Reserva do Sapal nature reserve. Keep your eyes skinned for storks and black-winged stilts. For a map of the reserve and leaflets on the rarer species of birds, ask at the reserve office, which is located within the castle. There is also a small museum in the castle which provides an overview of Castro Marim, past and present. Exhibits include spearheads, cannon balls, hunting traps, farming tools and explanations of the surrounding salt-pans and nature reserve. *Castle. Tel: 081 531134. Open: Monday to Friday 9am–5.30pm. Free.*

Location: Castro Marim is on the N122, 4km northwest of Vila Real de Santo António

Faro

*C*apital of the Algarve since 1756, and seat of authority since the 16th century, the city of Faro is the gateway for visitors by air to the whole region. The architecture of the city has been severely impoverished by sieges, raids and earthquakes. Ironically the worst damage was done by the British, long-standing allies of the Portuguese, when the Earl of Essex sacked the city (then under Spanish occupation) in 1596. Most of what was left was then wiped out by the catastrophic earthquake of 1755. In spite of all this the city manages to retain a charming old walled town at its heart and several noteworthy churches.

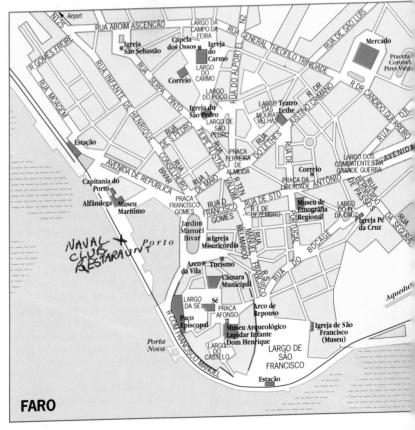

FARO

Sightseeing aside, Faro is a pleasant place for a leisurely stroll around the shady harbour-side gardens, for ambling through the old quarter or for shopping is the central pedestrianised streets (see page 30 for a suggested walk through the city).

Visitors to Faro in summer should make an early start; parking is notoriously difficult (try the area around the waterfront for the best chance of free parking) and sightseeing in the midday heat is no joke.

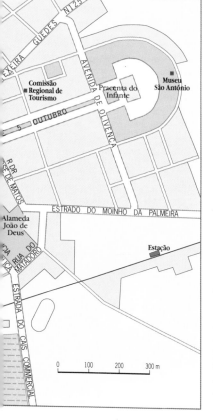

Comissão Regional de Tourismo

Praceta do Infante

Museu São António

CAPELA DOS OSSOS
(Chapel of Bones)

Tucked behind the Igreja do Carmo (see below) is the gruesome Chapel of Bones, faced with some 1,250 bones and skulls of monks and parishioners, dug up from the church graveyard. The chapel was built in 1816 and the story goes that the bishop of the city considered skulls and bones cheaper and more effective than bricks and mortar.

As in the equally grim but compelling Chapel of Bones in the Church of São Francisco, Évora (page 103), a haunting inscription in Portuguese warns of human mortality. *Largo do Carmo. Open: Monday to Saturday 10am–1pm, 3–5pm. Admission charge, pay in the sacristy of the Igreja do Carmo.*

IGREJA DO CARMO
(Carmelite Church)

Standing among blocks of modern flats in the Largo do Carmo square, the majestic twin-belfried façade of the Carmelite Church looks completely out of place. Even so, the interior of this fine baroque church is profusely decorated with 18th-century gilded woodcarvings. *Largo do Carmo. Open: Monday to Friday 10am–1pm, 3–5pm. Free.*

IGREJA DE SÃO FRANCISCO
(Church of St Francis)

Just west of the old town, the Igreja de São Francisco stands on a large desolate square. The exuberant gilded wood-carving, and the glazed tiles depicting scenes from the life of St Francis, provide a surprising contrast to the façade. *Largo de São Francisco. Open: no official opening hours (ring the bell on the door to the left of the entrance). Free.*

FARO

IGREJA DO SÃO PEDRO
(Church of St Peter)

São Pedro is embellished with beautiful baroque gilded woodwork and, in one of the chapels, *azulejo* tiles depicting St Peter. The 16th-century church was built on the site of a fishermen's chapel.
Largo de São Pedro. Open: daily 9am–1pm, 3–7pm. Free.

MUSEU ARQUEOLÓGICO LAPIDAR INFANTE DOM HENRIQUE (Prince Henry Archaeological Museum)

Archaeology apart, this museum should be seen for its exceptionally elegant Renaissance setting. It is located in the quiet two-tiered cloister of the former convent of Nossa Senhora da Assunção. The façade stands on the Praça Afonso III, next to the cathedral square. It is not immediately apparent that this is a museum but you will recognise the portico by the coat of arms which features a shrimping net.

Archaeological exhibits on the ground floor range from prehistoric to neoclassical, the star attraction being a large 3rd-century AD Roman mosaic of Neptune, which was dug up near the railway station. On the upper gallery of the cloister, the views of the gargoyles are more inspiring than the paintings and pottery on display.
14 Praça Afonso III. Tel: 089 822042. Open: Monday to Friday 9am–12.30pm, 2–5pm. Admission charge.

MUSEU DE ETNOGRAFIA
(Ethnographic Museum)

Situated on the third floor of an austere public building, the Ethnographic Museum is devoted to the traditional life of the Algarvians. Exhibits include tuna nets, chimney pots, beehives and basketry.
Rua do Pé da Cruz 4. Tel: 089 27610. Open: Monday to Friday 9am–5pm. Admission charge.

MUSEU MARITIMO
(Maritime Museum)

Faro's Maritime Museum, located on the seafront side of the harbour, houses a collection of model ships, nautical gear and a fascinating display of fishing equipment: tuna harpoons, cuttlefish traps, spider crab cages and many more methods for luring creatures from lagoon and sea.
Rua Capitania do Porto. Tel: 089 803601. Open: Monday to Saturday 9am–noon, 2–5.30pm. Admission charge.

SÉ (Cathedral)

On the main square of the old town, Faro's cathedral is a much-restored medley of Gothic, Renaissance and Baroque. Of the original church built in 1251, probably on the site of a former Moorish mosque, only the tower and portal survive. The interior is cool, spacious and relatively unadorned. The most impressive features are the 18th-century glazed tiles in the side chapels.
Largo de Sé. Open: Monday to Saturday 10am–noon, 3–5pm; Sunday only during services. Free.

Location: Faro is on the N125, 305km southeast of Lisboa (Lisbon) and 53km west of Vila Real de Santo António. Tourist office: 8 Rua da Misericórdia, by the Arco da Vila. Tel: 089 803604. Open: Monday to Friday 9.30am–8pm (7pm in winter); weekends 9.30am–12.30pm, 2–5.30pm.

LAGOA

Not to be confused with the larger town of Lagos, Lagoa lies on the main road east of Portimão. It is a small unpretentious town, known first and foremost as the Algarve's chief producer of wine.

There is nothing very remarkable about the town of Lagoa itself, though you can still find plenty of local atmosphere in the back streets, particularly in the tiny *tasca* bar-cum-grocery stores where the locals knock back Lagoan wines amid strings of hanging onions and crates of oranges. The town's main sight is the parish church with its restored baroque façade.

In the big Cooperativa on the main road, you can taste Lagoan wines and watch the processes of cork-fitting and label-pasting, still done by hand. Red wines predominate (and you will see bottles of it throughout the Algarve) but there is also a Lagoan white, a rosé and a golden sherry-like aperitif wine. Tasters should be wary of the high alcohol content of Lagoan wines – 13 or 13.5 degrees is quite normal.

The Lagoa Wine Cooperativa is on the Portimão road. Tel: 082 52557. Open: Monday to Friday 9.30am–12.30pm, 2–5.30pm. Free, but you pay if you taste the wines. Book 24 hours ahead.

Porches

The potteries of Porches are to be found along the N125, 5km east of Lagoa. Here you can find everything from ceramic snails to ornate Algarvian chimney-pots. For floral-patterned *majolica,* based on traditional designs, try Porches Pottery (on the south side of the main road). Here you can watch the pots and plates being painted by hand. There are countless more ceramics shops selling traditional and rustic pottery at lower prices.

Slide and Splash Water Park

One of several water parks in the Algarve, Slide and Splash lies on the N125 between Lagoa and Estômbar. It is a huge leisure park with corkscrew water shutes, a whirlpool, a waterfall and a river ride, providing hours of fun for all age groups.

Vale de Deus, Estômbar. Tel: 082 341685. Open: April to October, daily 10am–6pm. Admission charge.

Location: Lagoa is on the N125, 7km east of Portimão.

The restored baroque façade off the Igreja Matriz (Parish Church) set in an immaculate cobbled square in Lagoa

Lagos

*F*or two centuries the harbour town of Lagos was the capital of the Algarve. Henry the Navigator also had his headquarters here and it was to Lagos that ocean-going caravels returned, laden with sugar, grain and gold from Africa and the East Indies. In 1434, the explorer Gil Eanes left Lagos on his pioneering voyage round Cape Bojador leading to the discovery of northwest Africa. It was also from here, in 1578, that the fanatical King Sebastião set sail on his North-African crusade, which culminated in the disastrous battle at Alcácer-Quibir, when almost his entire army was destroyed, and with it the flower of the Portuguese aristocracy.

Today Lagos serves as a centre for the British, Dutch and German holiday-makers staying in the coastal resorts of the western end of the Algarve. Despite devastation by the 1755 earthquake, and more recently by the tidal wave of tourism, the town still has a certain elegance. The fort and part of the city walls still stand, the streets are cobbled and narrow and there are still some fine churches. This, combined with a cheerful abundance of restaurants, cafés, bars and shops, makes Lagos one of the most popular towns on the coast.

Most of the town's sights are within a short distance of the Praça da República (confusingly also called the Praça Infante Dom Henrique) where a large bronze statue of Henry the Navigator, sextant in hand, looks out to sea.

IGREJA DE SANTA MARIA
(Church of St Mary)

This 16th-century church was almost entirely restored in the 19th century. The finest features of the interior are the 18th-century wooden statues, including one of São Gonçalo, patron saint of Lagos. It was from the Manueline window of the church that King Sebastião is said to have roused his troops and bid a last farewell to the people of Lagos.
Praça de República. Open: only during Mass.

IGREJA DE SANTO ANTÓNIO
(Church of St Antony)

The sober façade of this small church hides the Algarve's most exuberant ecclesiastical interior. Known as 'the Golden Chapel', it has a profusion of carved and gilded woodwork, surrounding scenes from the life of St Antony. Miraculously, the main body of the church survived the 1755 earthquake, though the beautifully painted vaulted ceiling was rebuilt.
Rua Alberto de Silveiro. Open: Tuesday to Sunday 9am–12.30pm, 2–5pm. Closed Monday and holidays. Free.

MERCADO DOS ESCRAVOS
(Slave Market)

On the Praça da República, an arcade beneath the Lagos Customs House marks the original site of the only slave market in Portugal. During the days of

the great discoveries, hapless individuals
were brought back from Africa to Lagos
and sold off at this site. Today the
arcade has a happier function: it acts as
an alfresco art gallery.

MUSEU MUNICIPAL (Municipal Museum)

Adjoining the Igreja de Santo António,
this small museum is devoted to
archaeology, ethnography and religious
art. A section displaying pots, coins,
Roman mosaics and other local finds is
followed by a selection of things
Algarvian: lobster pots, fishing nets and
farming tools, plus a few freak animal
foetuses, including a two-headed cat and
a one-eyed sheep.

*Rua General Alberto de Silveira. Tel: 082
762301. Open: Tuesday to Sunday
9.30am–12.30pm, 2–5pm. Closed: Monday
and public holidays. Admission charge.*

Evening light in Lagos

Nearby beaches

The main beach is the long exposed
stretch of Meia Praia, northwest of the
centre. More picturesque, sheltered
(and crowded) are the cove beaches west
of town, tucked under golden cliffs. For
coastal scenery you cannot beat Ponta
da Piedade, a promontory where cliff
erosion has produced free-standing
pillars, stacks and arches. From the clifftop you can walk down a path to the
grottoes. Alternatively you can go all the
way in a fishing boat from the Lagos
waterfront.

*Location: Lagos is 19km west of Portimão,
34km east of Sagres. Tourist office: Largo
Marquês de Pombal. Tel: 082 763031.
Open: daily 9.30am–12.30pm, 2–5pm; but
closed weekends in winter.*

Loulé

*L*ocated northwest of Faro, set among orchards of fig, olive and orange trees, Loulé is one of the principal market towns of the Algarve. In a province where the artisan is becoming a dying breed, the town is one of the few genuine handicraft centres. Wander down back alleys north of the market and you can still hear the hammers of the coppersmiths beating pots and pans in small dim workshops.

To see Loulé at its best go on a Saturday morning when colourful market stalls spill into the streets around the mock-Moorish market building, Inside, wizened women, clad in black, squat by the walls, waiting to make a few *escudos* by selling a basket of eggs or a shoebox full of chicks. Locals take their pick from the fish and vegetable stalls, while tourists are lured by the cheap chunky pottery and the handmade hats and baskets. Outside, street stalls are stacked with local produce: bags of almonds, buckets of olives, bunches of herbs, crates of oranges and sausages in all shapes and sizes.

In the narrow cobbled streets of the centre, the Moorish origins of Loulé are still apparent. Modern shops may be taking over from artisans' workshops but many of them still specialise in the local handicrafts, such as baskets made from esparto grass, mule saddles, ironwork, leather goods, woodcarvings, lacemaking and earthenware vessels.

The big event of the year in Loulé is carnival. Crowds come from all over the Algarve to watch the colourful floats, the marching bands and the Battle of Flowers. The main religious procession is held two weeks after Easter when a statue of the town's patron saint, Nossa Senhora da Piedade, is taken back to her sanctuary in the 16th-century chapel (of the same name) which is set on a hill just to the west of Loulé.

CASTELO (Castle)

Possibly of Arab origin, Loulé's castle has been in Portuguese hands since 1249 when the remaining Moorish parts of the Algarve were reconquered. Little remains of the castle itself, but the restored walls and towers afford panoramic views of Loulé and the surrounding landscape. There is a small museum in the grounds with an interesting collection of artefacts.
Rua Paio Perez Correia. For information ring the town hall, tel: 089 415000. Open: Monday to Saturday 10am–5.30pm.

IGREJA MATRIZ (Parish Church)

The handsome Gothic parish church is easily distinguished by its lofty onion-domed bell tower. Inside there are some beautifully tiled chapels, notably the first on the right, depicting the *Nativity* and the first on the left depicting the *Adoration of the Magi*. The second chapel on the left has typically Manueline carvings. The main altar, in contrast to the idolatrous gilt stacks you see so frequently in the Algarve, is quite restrained, the main decoration being the *azulejos* on either side. The church stands on a square overlooking the charming, but oddly named, Jardim dos Amuados, or Sulky People's Garden.

Largo da Matriz. Open: normally 9am–11am. If closed try the priest's house at No 19 Calçada dos Sapateiros, the street to the right of the gardens as you face them.

IGREJA DE NOSSA SENHORA DA CONCEIÇÃO (Church of our Lady of the Immaculate Conception)

Close to the castle, this small church looks very simple from the exterior but it has an elaborate carved wooden altarpiece and walls that are almost entirely covered with 18th-century blue and white *azulejos*. The biblical scenes depicted include the *Presentation of the Virgin at the Temple*, the *Circumcision of Christ* and the *Adoration of the Magi*.

Rua Paio Perez Correia. Open: Monday to Saturday, 9am–6pm.

Location: Loulé is 18km northwest of Faro. Tourist office: Edifício do Castelo. Tel: 089 463900. Open: Monday to Friday 9.30am–8pm; Saturday, Sunday and off-season 9.30am–noon, 2–5.30pm.

A quiet corner in Loulé, a town renowned for its excellent shops selling local crafts and its colourful markets

Monchique

*T*he Serra de Monchique, forming a natural boundary between the Algarve and the Alentejo, is a thickly wooded mountain range covered with cork oak, eucalyptus, chestnut and pine. The lush and varied vegetation has given it the name of 'the garden of the Algarve'. The hillside roads are bordered by mimosa, wild rhododendron and the *Arbutus unedo* tree, whose strawberry-like berries are the main ingredient of *medronho*, the locally made, fiery liqueur.

The scenery and the views, combined with the attractions of a spa village and a hilltown, make Monchique one of the Algarve's most popular tourist excursions. Don't be surprised, therefore, if a coach descends mid-morning on the Caldas de Monchique, spilling out tourists and temporarily disturbing the tranquillity of this pretty spot in the valley.

CALDAS DE MONCHIQUE

The centuries-old spa town of Caldas de Monchique lies in a quiet, wooded valley, 250m above the coastline. The medicinal waters, discovered by the Romans, are said to do wonders for rheumatism, skin diseases, convulsions and indigestion. Even so, the dropsy-

The hilltown of Monchique

ridden King João II found their therapeutic value questionable when, in 1495, he bathed at Monchique (albeit against medical advice) and died shortly afterwards in Alvor. There are eight springs altogether, which produce 20 million litres of water a year, and if you don't take the waters here you are bound to taste them in bottled form somewhere along the Algarve.

Focusing on its main square, the resort consists of a few hotels and restaurants, a wine *bodega* and a converted casino, which looks like a Moorish palace. Gambling was popular with the Spanish bourgeoisie, who frequented the Caldas de Monchique in the mid-19th century. Now a handicrafts centre, the former casino sells pots of Monchique honey and bottles of *medronho* liqueur. Taste this before you buy, and be prepared for the kick; the *medronho* made locally is 90 per cent proof.

Beyond the square a babbling brook tumbles down the hillside. Stone picnic benches are laid out in the shade of the waterside trees, making an ideal picnic spot. From here there are lovely walks through the woods. Down the hill from the main square, you can try the waters of Monchique for yourself. Ailments aside, they are said to put years on your life. The warm waters are far from refreshing, however, and have an offputting odour. A nip of *medronho* is a sure antidote.

MONCHIQUE

The market town of Monchique lies 7km north of the Caldas, overlooking a valley of orchards and woods. It is traditionally a handicrafts centre and along the approach road you can see stalls selling basketry and pottery.

Formerly a pretty mountain village, Monchique has expanded somewhat inelegantly, the outskirts typified by dull modern architecture and by bulldozers, which continue to carve up the hillsides. However, the narrow, roughly cobbled alleys of the centre, a few still lined with elegant 18th-century houses, are well worth exploring. Moreover, the views from the upper levels of the town are breathtaking.

Every month (on the third Friday) Monchique is the scene of a huge agricultural fair when all the local farmers gather to trade their livestock.

Igreja Matriz (Parish Church)

The main church in Monchique is famous for its extraordinary Manueline portal. The carved twisted columns, resembling cables of rope, radiate out into nautical knots, creating a striking effect against the stunning white façade of the church. The interior, immaculately kept, has three naves supported by pillars with Manueline capitals and a fine wooden ceiling, while blue, white and yellow *azulejos* decorate the lower side walls of the church.
Rua da Igreja. Open: no official hours, but a keyholder lives near by.

Convento di Nossa Senhora do Desterro (Convent of our Lady of Sorrows)

This grey neglected convent, surrounded by camellias and weeds, perches above the town and can only be reached on foot. It is no more than a shell but it is one that commands a superb sweep of the Serra de Monchique, giving way to the coast below. The best views are from the bell tower, but watch out for falling debris as you go.

MONCHIQUE

Nearby

West of Monchique the road snakes up the side of the Fóia mountain through woods of eucalyptus and pine, which soon give way to scrub and moorland. Along the wayside, flower-decked restaurants tempt you with their sweeping views over hills and valleys to the coast and their alfresco meals of smoked ham and chicken *piri-piri*. Hidden on the hillsides are the villas and pools of an expatriate British community who, no doubt anticipating the tidal wave of tourism on the coast, built villas on the quiet slopes of Fóia in the 1950s and 1960s.

The peak of Fóia, which you expect to be totally deserted, is scarred by TV masts, tourist shops and hawkers. Stallholders do a roaring trade in chunky

Chairs painted with bright floral designs for sale in Monchique

sweaters, sold to tourists caught unawares by the cold gusts on the peak.

Provided that there is no mist or heat haze, the views will make your trip worthwhile. The peak, at 902m, is the highest in the Algarve and, on a clear day, you can see the foothills stretching all the way to Cabo de São Vicente (Cape St Vincent).

The peak of Picota, rising to the southeast of Monchique, has equally good, if not better, views, despite its more modest height (773m). There is no proper road to the top, but the hike up is well worth the effort.

Location: Caldas de Monchique is 18km north of Portimão. Monchique town is 25km north of Portimão.

MONTE GORDO

Close to the Spanish border, Monte
Gordo is the resort which smacks most
of the Spanish costas. Concrete blocks
predominate and the centre has none of
the fishing village charm so typical of the
majority of the Algarve resorts. Now that
Spain is linked to the Algarve by a bridge
across the Rio Guadiana, the number of
visitors has increased and recent
development has been substantial.

On the plus side, Monte Gordo has a
huge beach with pale golden sand and
the warmest waters along the Algarve
coastline. The boulevard running parallel
to the beach provides a variety of eating
places, from burger bars to restaurants
serving clam *cataplana* (casserole). Large
hotels and apartment blocks loom
behind the beach, with a hinterland of
sandy pinewoods providing some relief.

Night-life centres either around the
casino, which is right on the beach, or in
discos and late-night bars.

*Location: Monte Gordo is 5km west of Vila
Real de Santo António, 52km east of Faro,
close to the Spanish border. Tourist office:
Avenida Marginal, beside the*

The resort of Monte Gordo

*casino. Tel: 081 44495. Open: Monday to
Friday 9.30am–5.30pm or later, weekends
9.30am–12.30pm, 2–5.30pm.*

RESERVA NATURAL DA RIA FORMOSA

Occupying over 50km of shoreline,
from Faro to the Spanish border, the
Ria Formosa reserve is an
ornithologists' haven. The marshland,
salt-pans and sandbars attract a
huge variety of birdlife, both resident
and migratory. Watch out in particular
for waders, such as black-winged
stilts, avocets, ruffs and little egrets.

Kept in captivity in the reserve are
the last surviving Algarve 'poodles'.
These friendly creatures, looking
more like curly-haired mongrels than
poodles, were once used by local
fishermen for guiding fish into their
nets or catching them in their teeth.
The dogs have also been known to
save sailors and fishermen from
drowning in storms at sea.

Olhão

*T*he old quarter of Olhão, with its cube-shaped, flat-roofed houses and stepped terraces, looks remarkably like an African kasbah, and you could be forgiven for thinking that the Moors had left their mark here in ancient times. In fact, Olhão was only developed in the early 19th century; it was through commercial links with North Africa that the town developed this Arabic style of architecture.

Olhão was put on the map by a group of intrepid fishermen. In 1808 they sailed in a small boat across the Atlantic to Rio de Janeiro where they informed the exiled Portuguese monarch, King João VI that Napoleon's troops had been driven from his kingdom. As a reward the seashore village was raised to the status of a town and called Olhão da Restauração (of the Restoration). The fishing community expanded, canneries were established and, by the late 19th century, Olhão had become a busy port.

Olhão is still a major port today. It is not immediately appealing because of its sprawling modern outskirts and the continuing demolition of elegant 19th-century houses in the centre. However, the old fishermens' quarters, the fish market and the restaurants (serving some of the freshest fish in the Algarve) make it well worth a visit.

The flat-roofed 'cube houses' of Olhão, influenced by the Arabic architecture of North Africa

The two offshore islands (see below), linked to Olhão by ferry, are fringed with sandy beaches. The islands are un-developed and are particularly popular with independently minded travellers.

FISH MARKET

The fish and food markets are housed in distinctive red-brick turreted buildings on the seafront. The variety of fish and seafood sold here is amazing, from the humble sardine – taken away in bagfuls by local housewives – to the luxury lobster, which is whisked off by local restaurateurs as soon as the markets are open. Outside are fish hanging out to dry suspended on rows of wooden hangers. Sardines sizzle on charcoal grills all over the town and in some of the simpler restaurants you can eat as many as you like for a fixed price.
Avenida 5 de Outubro. Open: daily 7am–1pm. Closed: Sunday.

IGREJA DE NOSSA SENHORA DO ROSARIO (Church of Our Lady of the Rosary)

This large late-17th-century baroque church was built with donations from local fishermen. The main reason for a visit is the bird's-eye view from the belfry over the town's roof-tops, chimneys and TV aerials. Beware of the booming bells that chime on the hour.

To the rear of the church is a tiny open chapel, dedicated to Nossa Senhora dos Aflitos (Our Lady of the Suffering), where candles burn among wax *ex votos* of human legs, arms and faces. For years the wives of Olhão's fishermen have been coming here to pray for their men at sea.
Praça da Restauração. Open: 9am–noon, 4.30pm–7pm. Closed: Monday. For access to the belfry ask in the sacristy.

Boats at anchor, Olhão

ILHA DA ARMONA AND ILHA DA CULATRA

From June to September ferries run roughly every 1½ hours to Olhão's two offshore islands. The Ilha da Armona takes 15 minutes by ferry. The service is less frequent during the rest of the year. For the best beach you need to walk about 1km, to the far side of the island. On the Ilha da Culatra get off the ferry at the second stop, Furol, where there are sandy beaches.

Nearby

The pretty village of Moncarapacho lies 7km northeast of Olhão. The parish church has a finely carved Renaissance portal and, close by, the chapel of Santo Cristo is covered with decorative 18th-century *azulejos*. The adjoining museum has an idiosyncratic collection of archaeology and sacred art.

Location: Olhão is 9km east of Faro. Tourist office: Largo da Lagoa. Tel: 089 713936. Open: Friday to Monday 9.30am–12.30pm, 2.30–8pm; Tuesday to Thursday 9.30am–8pm with earlier closing in winter.

Portimão

A major fishing port and industrial centre, Portimão is the largest and busiest city in the Algarve. It has no ancient monuments and, until recently, was renowned for the worst traffic congestion in southern Portugal. It is hardly surprising therefore that most tourists keep their distance.

There are, however, several plus points to Portimão: they include the shopping centre (the best in the Algarve), the sardine cafés by the harbour, the bustling street life and – the most recent addition – a spectacular modern suspension bridge across the Arade river. Situated on the outskirts of the town, with splendid views of the estuary, the new bridge takes all the through traffic, giving a new lease of life to the centre.

The green parks of Portimão

The town's main tourist attraction used to be the harbour, where fish from the trawlers were tossed up in wicker baskets to the ice trays on the quayside. Sadly the catch is now landed on the other side of the estuary, where there is no public access. Even so, the harbourside is still a colourful spot where you may see the occasional trawler offloading sardines, a luxury yacht gliding in full of tourists or a big-game cruiser weighed down with shark.

Inland from the harbour the streets are always full of shoppers. Not far from the main church, the pedestrianised Rua do Comércio and the Rua Vasco da Gama are the principal shopping streets, selling fashionable clothes, food, furniture and all things Portuguese. In the rather more elegant Rua Santa Isabel, exclusive boutiques and a stylish art gallery occupy the ground floors of some of the town's finer houses. The old fish market in the centre has been turned into a gallery for contemporary art while a new fish market – one of the best in the Algarve – is located to the west of the centre.

By late morning the wafting smell of charcoal-grilled fish permeates the streets and the café-style restaurants on the waterside begin to fill. Here the dish of the day, every day, is the simple sardine, eaten alfresco with salad and a jug of wine. In more sophisticated places you can try fish soups, fish risottos or freshly grilled bream, bass, swordfish and *peixe espada,* the long skinny 'scabbard fish', which has a pointed snout and silvery scales.

IGREJA MATRIZ (Parish Church)

Dominating the centre of Portimão, the parish church was rebuilt after earthquake devastation. The finest surviving feature of the original church is the portico.
Largo da Igreja. Open: daily 9am–noon, 6–7pm.

LARGO 1° DE DEZEMBRO (1st of December Square)

The tiles on the benches in this small park are well worth studying because they vividly illustrate 10 crucial episodes in Portuguese history. The name of the park refers to 1 December, 1640, the date which marked the end of 60 years of Spanish rule.

Browsing in Portimão's market

Excursions

Yachts moored in the harbour offer coastal trips and big-game cruisers lure in fishing enthusiasts with their advertisements featuring spectacular photographs of sharks. Even if the sharks don't bite, there are plenty of sea bass, conger eels and ray. The cruisers are fully equipped with fighting chairs, big-game rods and the latest sonar systems which can detect fish up to a distance of 57km. No experience is necessary. Among the game species regularly caught are the blue shark, the copper shark and the streamlined mako, which is renowned for its speed, fighting instincts and sensational leaps from the sea. Rather more tasty than other local sharks, it has been known to turn up on tourist plates, under the guise of swordfish.

Location: Portimão is 62km west of Faro and 18km east of Lagos. Tourist office: Largo 1° de Dezembro. Tel: 082 23695. Open: Monday and Friday 9.30am–12.30pm, 2–7pm; Tuesday to Thursday 9.30am–8pm; weekends 9.30am–12.30pm, 2–5.30pm.

The crescent-shaped beach at Praia da Luz, one of the Algarve's best resorts

PRAIA DA LUZ

Praia da Luz is one of the most appealing beach resorts in the Algarve. Situated at the quieter western end of the Algarve, the resort is made up of villas, pools and gardens, built around a crescent-shaped sandy bay with development spreading over the low western headland. Despite its growth, Luz is still a relaxed, peaceful place to stay. The emphasis is on beach life, sports and eating out at night. For a resort of its size the sports facilities are impressive: windsurfing, sailing, water-skiing, diving, riding, tennis and squash.
Location: Praia da Luz is 10km west of Lagos.

PRAIA DA OURA

Once an offshoot of Albufeira, Praia da Oura has grown to become a self-contained tourist resort. Main attractions are the sandy beach, non-stop night-life and the bullring.
Location: Praia da Oura is 2.5km east of Albufeira centre.

PRAIA DA ROCHA

The pioneer resort of the Algarve, Praia da Rocha has been receiving tourists since the 1930s. Anyone who knew the resort in those days would find it hard to recognise today. From one elegant hotel and a handful of villas it has grown into an international resort with scores of modern hotels, bars and souvenir shops.

The prime attraction is, and always has been, the beach. This looks entirely natural, though in fact the sands were imported from nearby Portimão when the harbour was dredged. The wide band of flat golden beach, backed by high sandstone cliffs, stretches for 2km. Wind and water erosion has left freakish rock formations along the beach, sculpted into arches, tunnels, and – if you use your imagination – shapes resembling animals and human beings.

Well above the beach, the clifftop promenade runs eastwards as far as the fortress of Santa Catarina, built to defend Portimão. Today café tables are laid out within the fort and tourists can take advantage of the views across the estuary of the Arade river and down to the jetty, where anglers cast their lines. From the western headland the views of the coastline are even more spectacular.

Praia da Rocha's first hotel was the Bela Vista, converted from a turn-of-the-century mansion with Moorish overtones. Today it looks incongruous amid the modern concrete.

From Praia da Rocha you can take a boat westwards along the coast to Praia dos Três Irmãos. Alternatively you can walk there along the clifftop. Either way there are excellent views of the rugged cliffs and rock stacks.
Praia da Rocha is 2km south of Portimão and 64km west of Faro. Tourist office:

Avenida Tomás Cabreira. Tel: 082 22290.
Open: Monday and Friday 9.30am–
12.30pm, 2–7pm or 8pm; Tuesday to
Thursday 9.30am–8pm; weekends and off-
season 9.30am–12.30pm, 2–5.30pm.

QUARTEIRA

Quarteira is often cited as the ugly
duckling of the Algarve and it is not
difficult to see why. The former fishing
village has been swallowed up by a
joyless sprawl of tower blocks. The
saving grace is the long sandy beach, but
even this has its drawbacks, with the
hotels right behind and the occasional
concrete-mixer encroaching on the
sands. Despite this it is still a popular
resort, particularly among people from
Lisbon who like to rent or buy new
apartments here. One consequence is

that bullfights take place in Quarteira's
bullring every week during the summer.

On the road to Albufeira, 7km from
Quarteira, the Atlantic Water Park has
slides, rides and, in high season, shows
are put on by an Acapulco high-diving
team.

Atlantic Water Park, on the N125. Tel:
089 397282. Open: daily in summer
9.30am–6.30pm. Closed in winter.
Admission charge.

Location: Quarteira is 22km west of Faro,
26km east of Albufeira. Tourist office: 53
Avenida Infante Sagres. Tel: 089 312217.
Open: Monday to Thursday 9.30am–8pm;
Friday to Sunday and off-season
9.30am–12.30pm, 2–5.30pm.

Sunset over Praia da Rocha

BEACHES

For many people the main attraction of travelling to the south of Portugal will be the splendid beaches of the Algarve. Despite the often crass and insensitive development of tourist facilities along the coast, the beaches themselves are, on the whole, still impressive. The vast expanses of clean sand and clear water inevitably attract thousands of visitors. Whether swimming, exploring the bizarre sculptural formations of the cliffs or just lying in the sun attracts you, there are few more congenial places in which to enjoy these activities.

Most of the resorts have developed from small fishing villages and it is still common to see boats, complete with fresh catch, being pulled ashore through crowds of half-naked sunbathers. Most visitors tend to congregate

around the largest and most central beach of a resort, so that those who are seeking relative isolation will often be rewarded by a short walk from there. The Algarve also has several small islands, accessible by ferry or fishing boat whose outstanding beaches are less crowded than most others.

The beaches of the western Algarve and the Alentejo coast are very different. Much sandy shoreline exists but, in many cases, the beaches can only be reached along unsurfaced roads and tracks. These beaches, which are never really crowded, attract a different type of visitor – young people who relish the inaccessibility and the ferocity of the Atlantic, and surfing *aficionados* in search of that elusive, perfect wave.

Clean sand, warm clear waters and rocks sculpted by the waves and the wind

Sagres and Cabo de São Vicente

*O*n the wild and windswept Sagres peninsula, turbulent seas pound against the cliffs. The land is parched, while the trees are stunted and bent from the unrelenting Atlantic gales. Perhaps it is not surprising that this southwesterly tip of Europe was once thought to be the *Fim do Mundo,* the 'End of the World'.

The giant wind compass, Sagres Fort

Holy site

The Romans called Sagres the *Sacrum Promontorium,* or Sacred Promontory, and the only buildings found here then were shrines dedicated to the gods. In the 8th century, when the Muslims invaded Iberia, the relics of St Vincent, the 4th-century Christian martyr, were brought here for safekeeping. According to legend, sacred ravens kept a permanent vigil over the spot where the bones of the martyr were hidden, and when these relics were transferred to Lisbon, four centuries later, the birds flew with the ship all the way.

Henry the Navigator

It was in the town of Sagres that Henry the Navigator set up his famous school of navigation, mustering the great carto-graphers, astronomers and mariners of the day. Here, it is said, these experts pooled their knowledge to design the caravel, the small sailing vessel that was used to plot the routes that led to the great age of discovery.

SAGRES

Today Sagres is no more than a fishing

village made up of squat white houses. The liveliest and most colourful spot is the harbour where the lobster boats arrive and offload their catch, destined for the market and local restaurants. The seas around Sagres, and off the southwest coast, provide some of the best fishing grounds in Portugal. Boats laden with tackle and bait can be hired by the day. Alternatively you can take a boat trip to see the coast and nearby grottoes.

Beaches

The beaches of Sagres are windy and the seas can be rough. The Praia do Martinhal, 4km northeast of Sagres, is the most appealing, particularly if you like windsurfing. More sheltered is the pretty little beach of Beliche, below a converted fortress, on the road to Cabo de São Vicente.

Fortaleza (Fortress)

The walls of this huge fortress loom on the rocky headland at the southern tip of the Sagres peninsula. Today the most striking thing about the fortress is its setting, and the awesome circuit of walls skirting huge cliffs above dramatic seas. The original buildings were destroyed in part by Sir Francis Drake ('the English pirate' according to local brochures) who raided this coast in 1587 when Portugal was under Spanish occupation. Further devastation resulted from the earthquake of 1755. The latest damage inflicted on the site has been the destruction of some of the older buildings within the walls to make way for a modern box-like navigational museum, and the cementing over of the old stone walls. The scandal had national repercussions with the President ordering a public enquiry.

From Henry the Navigator's era, only a small white-domed chapel survives and this is always shut. Possibly original, too, is the gigantic *rosa dos ventos* or wind compass, which was discovered under a church in the 1920s and now stands to the left of the entrance.

From the tip of the promontory, where the red-topped lighthouse sits, you can watch fishermen precariously perched on the cliff ledges, dangling their long lines into the deep-blue seas below. Mists permitting, you can see the lighthouse of Cabo de São Vicente to the west and the coastline as far as Lagos to the east.

CABO DE SÃO VICENTE
(Cape of St Vincent)

By driving 6km over the wind-battered plateau from Sagres you will reach Cape St Vincent, which marks the very southwesterly tip of continental Europe. From the look-out point to the right of the lighthouse there are views of freighters and tankers rounding the Cape, and beyond them a seemingly endless ocean. The beam of the lighthouse is one of the most powerful in Europe, visible from a distance of 90km. If the lighthouse is open, you can climb up the spiral staircase to see the prisms and 3,000 watt bulbs. Outside, stalls sell fishermens' socks and sweaters to tourists shivering in T-shirts and shorts. Despite the wind, Cape St Vincent is one of the best places in southern Portugal to see wild flowers, especially between February and June. In addition, huge numbers of migrating birds use the Cape as a staging post between Europe and Africa in March, April, September and October.

Cabo de São Vicente lighthouse. Open: no official timetable – hours depend on the availability of the lighthouse keepers. Free.

HENRY THE NAVIGATOR

The initiative behind Portugal's spate of maritime expeditions and discoveries, which began in the 15th century and led to the development of the vast Lusitanian empire, is traditionally credited to Prince Henry, 'the Navigator'. The third son of King João I, he was rewarded for his part in the capture of the North African stronghold of Ceuta, in 1415, with the dukedom of Viseu and governorship of the Algarve. In 1418 he moved from Viseu to Lagos and established a school of navigation, either in the city or near Sagres – the exact location is not known. The school attracted the finest cartographers, astronomers and navigators of the age and contributed greatly to the improvement of navigational science.

That, at least, is the legend. In fact, Prince Henry was just as concerned to continue his assaults on Islamic North Africa, in the name of Christianity, as he was interested in voyages of discovery. He repeatedly defended Ceuta against Muslim attempts to recover it, he encouraged a disastrous attack on Tangier in 1437 and, as an old man, fought at the famous victory at Alcácer-Ceguer. Certainly many expeditions did set out from Lagos, including those of Gil Eanes, who sailed along the West African coast several times before rounding Cape Bojador, south of the Canary Islands, in 1434. Prince Henry also encouraged the settlement of the Atlantic islands. Madeira was discovered in 1419, the Azores in 1427 and the Cape Verde Islands in 1457.

The motivation for these voyages was partly religious but largely commercial. By the time of his death, in 1460, Henry had managed to win the monopoly of all trade, including slavery, conducted along the African coast south of Cape Bojador, as well as a substantial percentage of the lucrative wheat and sugar trade by then operating out of Madeira.

Statue of Henry the Navigator, Lagos

The fort at Sagres, close to the site of Henry the Navigator's residence and school

SAGRES

Fifteenth-century cannon at Sagres

Vila do Bispo

Some 9km northeast of Sagres, Vila do Bispo is a crossroads village with hilltop windmills and cafés serving *percebes* (barnacles), the local speciality. The parish church is decorated with particularly fine 18th-century *azulejos*.

West coast beaches

The wild beaches of the west coast of the Algarve are very different in character from those of the developed south coast. Wind, strong waves and difficult access keep away all but avid surfers and backpackers, leaving these dramatic beaches practically untouched by tourism. The first and most accessible beach, heading north from Sagres, is the Praia do Castelejo. This is well signposted from Vila do Bispo. *En route*, the Torre de Aspa, a natural rock formation, soars to 150m. At the beach

great rollers crash on to the sands and rocks. Watch them from the beach bar (where the *arroz de pesce* (fish with rice) is particularly good) or walk the clifftops for spectacular sea views.

Further up the coast, at the beaches of Amado and Bordeira, the sands, surf and cliffs are staggeringly beautiful. Apart from the odd surfer, all you are likely to see is a local goatherd coaxing his flock along the cliffs. Both beaches are reached by dirt tracks, lined by dusty cacti and windblown fig trees. There are no signs, so follow your nose or ask a local.

Location: Sagres is 33km west of Lagos on the N125 and N268. Tourist office: Promontório de Sagres. Tel: 082 64125. Open: Sunday and Monday 11am–5pm; Tuesday to Saturday 9.30am–7pm (to 5.30pm in winter).

SALEMA

Tucked away at the west end of the Algarve, the small village of Salema lies in the lee of the Sagres promontory. The main attraction here is the long sandy beach where the fishing community is still very much in evidence. In the early morning you can watch fishermen untangling their nets or slicing squid by the side of their brightly coloured fishing smacks.

Up from the beach, on the east side, a jumble of white flat-roofed houses make up the village. The narrow cobbled streets, where black-clad women gossip in doorways, have plenty of local character.

To the west, and climbing up the slopes of the valley, the development is distinctly modern. The Salema Beach Club, a favourite British haunt, is a spreading complex of villas and apartments, with restaurants, swimming pools and bars.

Among the beach activities on offer are waterskiing, swimming, windsurfing and pedalos. Alternatively you can take a trip along the coast in a fishing boat. The Parque da Floresta golf-course lies 3km inland, set in hilly country-side.

Nearby

Raposeira is the village where Henry the Navigator once lived – or so local tradition has it. Villagers will point you in the direction of his so-called house. The village was also a resting place for medieval pilgrims who came all the way from Mértola (in the Alentejo) to worship the relics of St Vincent at Sagres. History aside, Raposeira is a pretty little village of old, gently decaying houses and winding streets and paths.

On the road to Raposeira, 2km after Figueira, Nossa Senhora de Guadalupe is a delightful Romanesque/Gothic church, where Prince Henry is said to have prayed.

Some of the region's quietest beaches can be reached by taking the narrow and bumpy road south of Raposeira (sign-posted to Ingrina). Fork left for Zavial which, when the tide is out, is a glorious beach. Ingrina (fork left) has a campsite and tends to be more crowded. The least accessible beach, Barranco João Vaz, is a favourite spot for naturists.

Location: Salema is 17km east of Sagres and 22km west of Lagos.

Invitation to tour by fishing boat

Silves

*I*t is hard to believe that this sleepy backwater, beside the Arade river, was once a sumptuous Moorish stronghold. As the capital of what was then called *al Gharb,* Silves was described by one historian as 'stronger and ten times more remarkable than Lisbon'. Likened to Baghdad, it was a city of mosques, bazaars and orchards full of citrus fruits. Ships used to come up the Arade river, anchor at the port and load up with lemons, oranges, figs and cork.

Christian Reconquest

In 1189, Sancho I brought this lavish stronghold to its knees. Furthering his anti-Muslim military campaign, he persuaded the Crusaders to help him expel the Moors from the citadel of Silves. The Moors held out for many months, but when the water in the cisterns had run dry and the silos were empty, they were forced to surrender. Despite Sancho's protestations, the Crusaders then plundered the castle, torturing and murdering the departing Moors.

Silves was recaptured by the Moors two years later but the writing was on the wall for Arab hegemony in the Algarve. By 1249, the capital had finally fallen, along with Faro and the other remaining Moorish footholds in the Algarve.

Silves gradually slipped into oblivion. By the late 16th century, the bishopric of the Algarve had moved from here to Faro and the population of this former capital was reduced to a mere 140.

Silves today

The fruit trees still flourish in modern Silves, but the Arade river is silted up and has been for centuries. The most prominent reminder of Silves' illustrious past is the noble shell of the Moorish fortress which crowns the town. Within the walls, the gardens provide an oasis of peace, except during the third week of July when the castle becomes the venue for an international beer festival.

Beneath its castle, Silves is a small and unassuming town of steep cobbled streets and red-roofed white- and pastel-washed houses. Away from the main sights you will see chickens scratching at the cobbles and housewives gutting fish in the streets, while the men congregate at shady benches or at the bar off the central square.

CASTELO (Castle)

The great circuit of turreted castle walls dominates the town. The steep cobbled Rua da Sé leads up, past the cathedral, to the arched gateway of the castle. Within the walls cats doze in the shade of jacaranda and apricot trees while stallholders sell linen and lace. The monumental bronze statue of Sancho I, inscribed 'King of Portugal, Silves and the Algarve' evokes memories of less tranquil days.

The castle battlements command sweeping views of Silves and the surrounding hills, covered in orange and lemon trees. Below you, to the south, is one of the town's last surviving cork factories. More immediately below are the old silos and the dark depths of the Cistern of the Dogs, created from an ancient copper mine. An underground

passage once linked the cistern to the Arade river and water was drawn up in clay buckets.
Largo da Castelo. Open: daily 9am–6pm. Free.

CRUZ DE PORTUGAL (Cross of Portugal)

On the outskirts of town, this carved cross, in a little pavilion, dates from the 16th century. It is 3m tall and carved from limestone. One side depicts the *Crucifixion,* the other the *Descent from the Cross.* From this side of town there are excellent views of the fortress.
On the N124 towards São Bartolomeu de Messines.

MUSEU MUNICIPAL DE ARQUELÓGIA (Municipal Archaeology Museum)

Opened in 1990, this innovative museum focuses on a beautifully preserved 12th-century Moorish well, which was discovered in 1979. During the excavation of the well, the diggers unearthed a wealth of artefacts, including ceramics, square Moorish coins and jewellery. Other exhibits, dating from the prehistoric era to the 17th century, include a carved head, which probably came from a Greek temple, Roman carvings and Phoenician and Visigothic pottery.
Rua das Portas de Loulé 14. Tel: 082 444832. Open: Monday to Saturday (except holidays) 10am–12.30pm, 2.30–6pm. Admission charge.

SÉ DE SANTA MARIA (Cathedral of Santa Maria)

Lying in the shadow of the castle, this cathedral is one of the Algarve's very few Gothic monuments. Like the rest of Silves, it has suffered the ravages of time

and undergone heavy restoration, but the dignified interior, with its lofty aisles and nave, is impressive nevertheless. Among the finest features are the tombs, some of which may belong to the Crusaders who helped capture Silves from the Moors in 1242.
Largo da Sé. Open: daily 9am–6pm in summer. Off-season closed for lunch Monday to Friday, Saturday morning and all day Sunday. Free (voluntary contribution).

Nearby

Some 10km northeast of Silves the peaceful Barragem do Arade reservoir makes an ideal spot for picnics, watersports or walks in the hills.

Location: Silves is 17km northeast of Portimão, on the N124. Tourist office: Rua 25 de Abril, off the Praça do Municipio. Tel: 082 442255. Open: Monday to Thursday 9am–8pm; Friday to Sunday and in winter 9.30am–5pm.

Silves – the central square

Tavira

*T*he town of Tavira, not far from the frontier with Spain, has an elegance rarely found in the Algarve. Straddling the Gilão river (which upstream becomes the Ségua), it is a town with handsome 18th-century houses and a skyline pierced by castle ramparts, plus the domes and spires of over 20 churches. Compared to towns west of Faro there is a refreshing absence of unsightly development.

Elegant Tavira beside the Gilão river

History

Formerly an Arab settlement, Tavira was conquered in 1242 by King Paia Peres Correira in revenge for the death of seven Christian knights who were killed by the Moors, during a truce, while they were out hunting near the town. Tavira later became a major port but the plague of 1645 drastically reduced its population. Subsequent earthquake damage and the silting up of the port led to its economic decline.

For centuries Tavira's mainstay was tuna fishing. Until the 1970s, by when stocks were severely depleted, tuna were trapped in nets, killed by a team of harpooners and hoisted aboard the boats. These bloody battles between tuna fish and harpooners were aptly described as 'bullfights of the sea'.

Tavira today

Tavira still has a prosperous air and retains some of its fine classical façades. On the south side of the river, gardens with palms run alongside the water as far as the covered market. Behind the green wrought-iron gates are stalls selling oranges and lemons, almonds, olives and figs, all from the fertile farmlands of the Sotavento (the leeward coast of the Algarve, stretching from Faro to the Spanish border). The far end of the market is given over to fish and seafood, much of it bought by the fish restaurants by the quayside. Upstream the arched stone bridge has Roman foundations. A plaque on the south side commemorates the bravery of the locals when they repelled the invading troops of King Juan I of Castile between 1383 and 1385.

Annoyingly, Tavira's churches do not have official opening hours. You must either visit when there is a service on, or track down the local keyholder by knocking on nearby doors and asking for *o chave* (the key).

CASTELO (Castle)
The castle is reached by means of a cobbled alley that leads up from the main square, the Praça da República. All that remains of the castle are the walls, but from the neighbouring gardens there are good views of the river and of Tavira's roof-tops and churches.
Open: daily 9am–5.30pm. Free.

IGREJA DO CARMO (Carmelite Church)
The plain exterior belies a baroque extravaganza of gilded carved woodwork.

Catching up on the gossip in Tavira

Particularly fine are the 18th-century chairs of the choir.
Largo do Carmo. Open: by obtaining the key from No 22, opposite the church.

IGREJA DA MISERICORDIA (Church of Mercy)
This church is only open for concerts but, from the outside, you can admire the very finely carved Renaissance portal dating from the 1540s. The interior has fine *azulejos* and gilded woodwork.
Rua da Galería.

IGREJA DE SANTA MARIA DO CASTELO (Church of Santa Maria of the Castle)
This simple whitewashed church, beside the castle ramparts, stands on the ruins of a former mosque. It was built in the 13th century but reconstructed after the 1755 earthquake. The church contains the tombs of King Paio Peres Correia and the Sete Caçadores, the seven Christian knights massacred by the Moors, thus precipitating the reconquest of the town.
Open: daily 10am–12.30pm, 2–5pm.

Nearby beaches
The best beaches are on the Ilha de Tavira, an offshore sandspit stretching for 11km. Buses link the centre of Tavira with the ferry landing stage about 2km away. Ferries land at the eastern tip of the island which, at this point, is crowded and unappealing – for a decent stretch of beach you must walk further along the shore.

Location: Tavira is 30km east of Faro and 23km west of the Spanish border. Tourist Office: Rua de la Galería 9. Tel: 081 22511. Open: daily 9.30am–8pm (5.30pm in winter).

VALE DO LOBO

Vale do Lobo – literally 'the Valley of the Wolf' – could hardly be less aptly named. Far from the image of a lean, hungry beast howling in the moonlight, this is an enormous, purpose-built holiday estate of over 750 luxury villages, most of them with their own swimming pool.

Within the low-rise, up-market complex there are three golf courses, the Roger Taylor Tennis Centre (where amateurs from all over Europe come to have their games reconstructed in intensive tennis courses), numerous other sporting facilities, banks, boutiques, beauty salons and restaurants and discos galore.

Hundreds of water sprinklers keep the resort's grounds as green and manicured as an English croquet lawn, while gardeners tend exotic shrubs, silent beneath their straw hats. The well-heeled tourists who strut about in the trendiest of leisure wear serve as a reminder of what the whole of the Algarve could have been like if the policy of developing it as a premium holiday destination had not been abandoned in the 1970s in favour of the fast buck.

There is no village of Vale do Lobo other than the tourist resort, which was originally developed in the late 1960s on farmland. Ironically, however, there is far more Algarvian character here than in the nearby resorts of Quarteira, Albufeira and Armação de Pêra, with their high-rise apartment blocks and fish 'n' chip shops. The highly civilised whitewashed villas of Vale do Lobo are all in the traditional Moorish style, with arched windows and doorways, lattice-work balconies and low, rounded chimneys topped with tiles.

Vale do Lobo suits holiday-makers for stylish, ritzy relaxation – especially people who want to throw in a bit of sport. If you want to enjoy the sand and sea, however, there is no alternative but to forsake this elite paradise for the public beach.

Location: Vale do Lobo is 15km west of Faro off the N125.

Vila Real – rebuilt as a model town after 1774 and influenced by Lisbon

VILA REAL DE SANTO ANTÓNIO

Washed away by the waves in the 17th century, Vila Real de Santo António rose again like a phoenix in 1774. It took just five months to rebuild, due largely to the ingenuity of the Marquês de Pombal, Chief Minister to King José. The town was constructed as a model fishing port, designed with the same grid pattern of streets and uniform façades as the Baixa quarter of Lisbon, which Pombal had reconstructed after the 1755 earthquake.

Today, Vila Real is best known as the principal border town between the Algarve and Spain. Located on the western shores of the Rio Guadiana it faces the small Spanish town of Ayamonte across the water. Just 6km upstream a handsome international bridge spans the Guadiana, creating a new road link with Spain and increasing the flow of traffic into southern Portugal.

The 18th-century houses in the centre give the town a certain elegance, though this is partially spoilt by an over-abundance of souvenir and T-shirt shops catering for Spanish day-trippers.

Vila Real de Santo António

Although tourism has taken over from fishing as the main money-spinner, tuna fish are still processed here and local fishermen supply their catch to the morning market.

In the centre, the Praça do Marquês de Pombal is a handsome square, paved black and white and bordered by well-proportioned 18th-century houses. On the river, ferries ply to and from Spain, patrol boats snoop around the waters and wading birds nose in the mud. The ferry crossing is cheap and fun, but Ayamonte itself is no more than a very ordinary border town. The ferry service operates every half hour (from 8–8.30am until 11pm or to 7.30pm in winter). Day cruiser trips along the scenic Guadiana river operating twice a week are well worthwhile (tel: 081 422220).

Location: Vila Real de Santo António is 53km east of Faro, on the border with Spain. Tourist office: off the Avenida da República, by the ferry terminal. Tel: 081 43272. Open: daily 8am–7.30pm.

Vilamoura

*S*aid to be the biggest holiday development in Europe, Vilamoura is an entirely purpose-built resort, covering around 1,600 hectares of coastal plain. There is no real centre and no real Portuguese charm. What it does offer is a great range of accommodation and a choice of sporting and leisure facilities.

Large tower blocks, in colours of pink, yellow and blue, make the central area look like a giant Legoland. Centred around the marina are multi-storey apartments and luxury 4- and 5-star hotels, complete with private Jacuzzis and heated pools. Further out, and stretching for several kilometres, are the ever-expanding clusters of new property complexes, somewhat misleadingly called 'villages'. These are made up of villas, apartments and sports facilities. Some of the most luxurious villas, kitted out with stereo, satellite TV and air-conditioning, are set among pine trees beside a golf-course. Despite the gargantuan proportions of the resort, construction still goes on. Half-built apartments are a familiar sight and will be until the target of 55,000 beds is reached. The figure currently stands at 35,000. The other target is self-sufficiency. Vilamoura already has its own herd of cattle.

What to see and do

If there is a centre to Vilamoura it is the 1,000-berth marina. The largest in southern Europe, this is a showcase for floating gin palaces, ritzy yachts and ocean-going clippers. There are yacht

Vilamoura's fine marina

The old quarter of Vilamoura

Sports facilities

For sports enthusiasts, Vilamoura has the best choice in the Algarve. There are no less than four 18-hole golf-courses, spaced around the outskirts of the resort. The favourite is the oldest, Vilamoura I, laid out over gently sloping hills with tree-lined fairways. Among other sports you can try tennis, riding, sailing, windsurfing, waterskiing and scuba diving. Clubs offer lawn bowling, clay-pigeon shooting, badminton and aerobics. Vilamoura is also the venue for some big sporting events, including sailing regattas and parachuting championships.

Night-life

The evening activities focus on restaurants, bars and the casino. Here you can try your hand at roulette, blackjack or French bank. Added attractions are live shows and a restaurant within the casino.
Tel: 089 302999. Open: 7pm–1am. Admission charge to the gaming room. Take your passport.

Nearby beaches

One of the least crowded beaches is Falésia, which stretches for several kilometres to the west of Vilamoura. Despite some development on the cliffs above, you can always find stretches of near-deserted sand. Beyond a promontory at the west end, the Olhos de Agua is a small beach surrounded by cliffs. The fishing community here is still very much in evidence but so are the tourists, some of them spilling over from Albufeira.

Location: Vilamoura is 26km west of Faro. Tourist office: in Quarteira, 4km away (see page 75).

trips along the coast or fishing excursions for big game.

The older and slightly more attractive quarter of Vilamoura focuses on the beach. Behind, on the main esplanade, waiters vie to draw tourists in to their restaurants. Food in Vilamoura ranges from Chinese take-away to lobster *cataplana* (casserole).

Vilamoura may be man-made but it is not without a history. The ancient remains across the road from the marina are clear evidence that there were Roman, Visigothic and Moorish settlements here. Excavations have revealed the foundations of a Roman patrician's house and the remnants of fine mosaics. A small museum near by contains all the finds from this site, including Roman lamps and Visigothic coins.
Cerro de Vilamoura. Tel: 089 312153. Open: daily 10am–8pm (5pm in winter).

The Alentejo

*T*he Alentejo - literally 'beyond the (river) Tejo' – is a vast, rolling, sun-baked plain; it is bordered, to the east, by a long backbone of craggy hills which form a natural frontier with Spain and, to the west, by the Atlantic. Southwards are the throbbing tourist resorts of the Algarve, the huge majority of whose visitors never venture more than a few kilometres inland.

Yet, just a couple of hours drive from the hotel-lined sandy beaches and manicured greens of the Algarve, there is some of the least-explored country in the Iberian Peninsula. Birds of prey soar over plains of cork oak forest and olive groves; hilltops are crowned by Moorish castles and whitewashed medieval villages. Streams and occasional lakes break up the landscape, which is carpeted with flowers in spring, before turning brown and barren as the hot, dry summer sets in.

The region, which for administrative purposes is divided into the twin provinces of Alto (Upper) and Baixo (Lower) Alentejo, encompasses a third of the total area of Portugal, although only about a tenth of the country's population lives there. Its hinterland has a slow, little-changing pace of life which neither gets, nor expects, many visitors.

There are some majestic *pousadas* (state-run hotels) serving as the only alternative to otherwise very basic accommodation, but these are few and far between. As a result there are some gloriously wild, arcane and far-flung places waiting to be discovered by anyone prepared to do some careful planning. Although many of the larger towns can be visited by road or rail, a car really is essential for discovering the

secrets of the Alentejo. Unless you like it roastingly hot, spring and autumn are the best times to visit.

It has been suggested that the 21st century will see leisure parks in the Alentejo, with watersports on artificial lakes, irrigated golf-courses, luxury hotels and helicopters whirring to and fro. Until then, hilltop towns like Monsaraz and Estremoz can expect their amazing views to change only with the seasons.

ALCÁCER DO SAL

From Moorish times to the present day, the purest salt in Portugal has been extracted from the marshy land on either side of the flood-prone Sado river, which the main EO1/N20 crosses at Alcácer do Sal. The drawbridge, which once allowed small ships up to the saltworks, is nowadays permanently down. Rice, wheat and vegetables are also grown on the flat, fertile land which surrounds this historic and attractive little whitewashed hilltop town, making it an important agricultural hub.

Many motorists stop by the bridge to watch the numerous storks, which feed in the rice paddies and circle over the town before returning to their nests; these look like huge baskets perched on the tops of churches and the town's taller houses, many of which have plants and weeds growing among their tiles. Dominating the medieval kernel at the town's heart is the 12th-century castle, built on the foundations of an earlier Moorish fortress.

Within the walls is the small, dark and atmospheric Santa Maria (a 12th-century church which can provide a cool escape from the summer heat) and the 16th-century Aracelli convent. The 16th-century Santiago church, below the castle, is beautifully tiled in antique *azulejos.* Another church of this era, the Espirito Santo, houses a small archaeological museum exhibiting scraps of Roman, Phoenician and Moorish pottery among a collection of motley artefacts found in the area. If you already know your history of the Alentejo, this museum will add a few interesting illustrations.

Location: Alcácer do Sal is in the northwest corner of the Alentejo, 52km southeast of Setúbal.

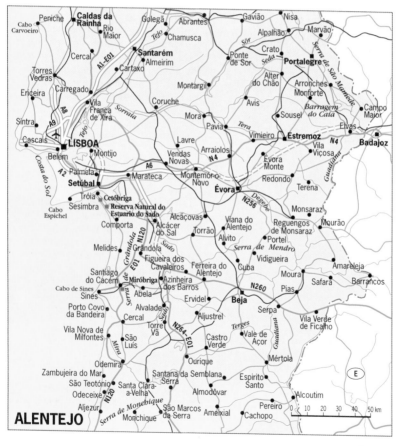

ALENTEJO

Barragem do Roxo dam. In the early evening, in particular, the Alentejo light can be crystal clear and the scattered villages stand out dazzlingly white in the wide open landscape.
Open: all day. Free.

Museu da Mina (Museum of Mining)

This interesting museum weaves together the geology and history of the area. It shows how Aljustrel lies at the end of a long belt of copper, stretching over to the great mines of Rio Tinto and Tharsis in Spain. The Roman Empire's insatiable demand for bronze (an alloy of copper and tin) led them to exploit these reserves on a scale which has never been seen since. Roman mining tools are on display, along with explanations of how they extracted the metal from the ore. Remains from the large Roman necropolis near by are also on show.
Tel: 084 601461. Open: all day. Free.

Nossa Senhora do Castelo

A long stone staircase, worn smooth over the centuries by the feet of innumerable pilgrims who have climbed to the top to do penance and pray for intercession by the blessed Virgin, leads to this small convent and shrine. In the early days, following the expulsion of the Moors, it stood as an important symbol of the victory of Christians over the infidel.
Open: all day. Free.

Location: Aljustrel is 36km southwest of Beja on the N263.

A blend of Moorish and classical architecture in Aljustrel

ALJUSTREL

Bang in the middle of the Alentejo, Aljustrel has been an important centre of industry ever since the Romans discovered extensive reserves of copper in the area. The town itself is not particularly impressive, but there are three principal attractions here.

Castelo (Castle)

This is one good reason for breaking your journey in Aljustrel. The castle is an unrestored ruin crowning a hill, but good for wandering around unmolested by truculent tour guides. The climb up is rewarded with great views of the surrounding countryside, over cork oak forest, cattle pasture and the blue water of a spindly shaped lake created by the

ALVITO

As you approach Alvito across the expansive outlying plains, it appears as a classic little castle-crowned, red-tiled Alentejan town ringed by whitewashed walls. Alvito is a characteristically sleepy place, where stubbly chinned old men pass the time of day sitting on benches, and the women are nowhere to be seen. Yet the town has a dazzling history, which is reflected in the rich atmosphere; this can be experienced by wandering the streets full of houses decorated with curvaceous arabesque ornament and by gazing up at the sturdy medieval castle.

The builders of Alvito's castle were the Barons of Alvito who, for centuries, were among the most powerful of Portugal's aristocracy. Their castle was completed in 1482, shortly after the king had created this the first Barony in the country; he also allowed the first Baron of Alvito the unprecedented honour of owning his own castle – until then every castle in Portugal was the property of the king.

Unlike other forbidding fortresses of this era, Alvito castle has, as well as defensive towers and crenellated parapets, a splendid Great Hall and several rooms with stone-carved arched windows. These were built for the benefit of the kings and queens of Portugal, who were regular guests at Alvito. One king, Manuel I, died here in 1521. The Barony declined over the centuries and Alvito castle fell into dereliction. Following imaginative and painstaking restoration, it re-opened as an atmospheric 20-bedroom *pousada* in September 1993. It makes a superb stop for anybody passing through this frequently forgotten little town.
Location: Alvito is 10km south of Viana do Alentejo and 28km north of Ferreira do Alentejo on the N257.

Alvito – a classic little Alentejan town of sleepy streets and quiet squares

Beja

*W*hen the national weather forecast is shown on Portuguese television, Beja almost invariably stands out as having recorded that day's highest temperature. The capital of Baixo (Lower) Alentejo, Beja is a dusty town at the hub of the region's expansive plains of wheat fields, cork oak forests and olive groves. In spring you approach the town along roads lined with poppies, with carpets of bluebells beyond; by high summer the land has been scorched into an endless brown.

Beja is not a place to spend time absorbing Alentejan atmosphere. It is an uncharacteristically busy town whose prosperity is underlined by super-markets, brimming shops and smart modern buildings. However, anybody who is trying to get under the skin of the region's history and culture should visit Beja, if only to visit the Convento da Nossa Senhora da Conceição. Another ruined convent, Convento de São Francisco, is being rebuilt and is due to open as a 37-bedroom *pousada*.

CASTELO (Castle)

There's not much left of the 40 towers which formed the outer walls of this massive fortress, built by King Dinis in the 14th century. However, the rather

Beja's castle keep

fine ivy-clad courtyard and keep are still there. An enthusiastic attendant shows visitors round, insisting that this was once one of the most impenetrable castles in Europe; if a besieging army had ever got in, the soldiers would surely have been burned to death by boiling oil poured on them from the gallery atop the 40m-high keep. A spiral staircase leads to this gallery, from where there is a fabulous view over the plains beyond the town. There is also a small military museum in the courtyard, which is worth a quick look.

Largo do Lidador. Tel: 084 23693. Open: 10am–noon, 2–6pm. Admission charge weekdays but free on Sunday.

CONVENTO DA NOSSA SENHORA DA CONCEIÇÃO

This 15th-century convent is one of the most beautiful buildings in the Alentejo, and an excellent example of the transitional style of architecture between Gothic and Manueline. The convent was among the wealthiest in Portugal and has a fine Sala do Capítulo (chapter house) and stone-carved cloisters decorated with some of the finest 15th-century *azulejo* tiles to be found anywhere in Portugal. The chapel is fronted by a baroque altarpiece of carved and gilded wood. It also has a serene atmosphere and is worth pausing in for a few minutes, especially if you are lucky enough to have it to yourself.

There is a rather disparate museum within the convent; this exhibits Roman coins and mosaics found on the site, a few bits of treasure dating from the convent's wealthy heyday (including a large Ming-dynasty bowl) and a strange tomb built in the shape of a barrel, apparently for a wine-maker. There is also a small collection of 16th-century paintings, including the Flemish breast-feeding *Our Lady of the Milk.*
Largo Nossa Senhora da Conceição. Tel: 084 23351. Open: 9.45am–12.30pm, 2–5.15pm daily, except Monday and public holidays. Admission charge.

Location: Beja is on the N260, 27km west of Serpa. Tourist office: 25 Rua do Capitão J F de Sousa. Tel: 084 23693.

THE PASSIONATE NUN
The most famous resident of the Nossa Senhora de Conceição convent was Sister Mariana Alcoforado. She had a furious love affair with a French Count who came to live in Beja during the war which Portugal fought with Spain between 1661 and 1668.

The erotically pious letters she wrote to him after his departure were, putatively, those published in French in 1669 as *Letters of a Portuguese Nun.* Her cell has a barred window through which she and the count are said to have made love (in the old-fashioned sense of the phrase); this has been reconstructed and attracts a great deal of prurient interest.

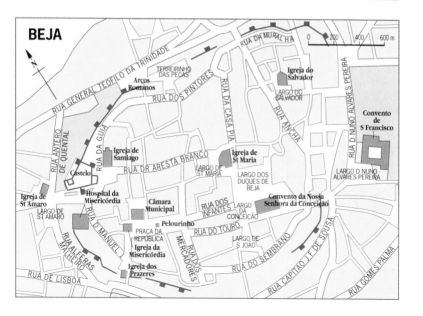

BEJA

Old Elvas, across the road, could not form a more striking contrast. Within the redoubtable ramparts, broken only by sturdy stone gateways, are cobbled streets, low arches and quaintly tumbledown whitewashed houses with iron-grilled windows and pots of flowers standing outside. Over centuries of hostility with Spain, strategic Elvas became known as *o chave do reyno* – 'the key to the kingdom' – and its formidable fortifications were no mere gesture of defiance: in 1644, during the War of Restoration, and again in 1659, Elvas withstood massive Spanish assaults. In 1801, it was despite the successful resistance of Elvas that the Portuguese capitulated to Spain after the Spanish had declared war over Portugal's refusal to break her alliance with the British. Ten years later, Wellington launched his siege of Badajoz from Elvas.

The joy of the old town is that it is still very much a lived-in quarter, with washing hanging up to dry, children playing football in ancient courtyards and drivers hooting furiously as they get stuck in impossibly narrow entrances. Sights not to miss are the 16th- and 17th-century Aqueduto da Amoreira (Amoreira Aqueduct) which brought water to the town from 7.5km away, the marble pillory in the triangular Largo Santa Clara, the mosaic paving in the Praça da República main square and the views over to Spain from the top of the ramparts, next to the castle.

Location: Elvas is on the N4 road 10km from Lisbon to Madrid. Tourist office: Praça da República, by the bus stop. Tel: 068 622236.

The Armoreira Aqueduct, near Elvas

ELVAS

Just 10km from the Spanish border, Elvas has the feel of a frontier town. Spanish car number plates are ubiquitous and prices are quoted in *pesetas* as well as *escudos*. The scruffy, nondescript new part of town is stuffed with restaurants where motorists travelling between Madrid and Lisbon stop for their first (or last) meal for which they pay Portuguese rather than (the much higher) Spanish prices.

ESTREMOZ

A day or two spent in fortified, hilltop Estremoz is likely to prove one of the highlights of a visit to southern Portugal (for a walking tour of the town see page 26). Estremoz has an ancient, otherworldly feel. No visitors experience this more intensely than those who stay in the grandiose 13th-century royal castle at the uppermost part of town; this has now been turned into the Pousada da Rainha Santa Isabel (tel: 068 22618; reservations essential). The rooms in this national monument are an extraordinary blend of the sumptuous and the spartan; there are enormous four-poster beds and bathrooms of marble quarried from the hills near by, as well as expanses of bare stone wall with lanterns hanging from ceilings high above. Even if you are not staying at the *pousada*, the reception staff will probably be happy to show you around; if not, you should at least climb the great marble staircase from the cavernous hall – the views from the dining room out over the plains of the Alentejo, are stupendous.

Rising above the royal palace is the castle keep, with its white marble 'Tower

Lago do Gadanha (Scythe Lake), Estremoz

Bargain hunting in the early morning market at Estremoz

of the Three Crowns' (a trio of kings all contributed to its construction). A steep, worn staircase leads up to a gallery from where you can see Évora, across the plains, and over to Spain in the east. Also in the castle is the enchanting Rainha Santa Isabel Chapel, bedecked with *azulejo* tiles depicting the life of this generous queen and saint who died in Estremoz in 1336, after devoting her life to the poor.

Open: keep and chapel, daily 9–11.45am, 2–5.45pm, except Monday and public holidays. Admission charge.

Location: Estremoz is 44km northeast of Évora and 57km south of Portalegre. Tourist office: 26 Largo da República. Tel: 068 333541.

FARMING

After the Christian Reconquest of southern Portugal, in the late 14th century, the land was divided up into large estates, or *latifundios*, centred around an isolated farm called a *monte*. In the Alentejo this system still prevails; the region supports itself almost entirely by agriculture and, indeed, is known as 'the granary of Portugal'. Cereal crops are grown in its most fertile areas, near to the coast and around the mountains of the northwest. The flat plains of the centre of the region are used for grazing large herds of cattle, sheep and pigs.

Forests of cork oak help break up the monotony of the landscape. Portugal is still the world's largest producer of cork. The difficult task of stripping the bark, without damaging the trunk, takes place in midsummer – but only after the tree has matured for about 25 years. The

Scenes from Portuguese rural life

trees live for just over 150 years and are stripped at three-yearly intervals, revealing the dark orange of their exposed trunks.

In the Algarve the cork oak is most commonly found on the slopes of the Serra de Monchique where there are also plantations of olive, pine and eucalyptus. Around Monchique itself you will see the *medronho,* or strawberry tree *(Arbutus unedo),* whose berries are made into a potent spirit, called *Aguardente de Medronho,* best drunk in small doses.

South of the mountains, the limestone region, called the Barrocal, produces olives, almonds in plenty and carob, whose oil-rich beans are exploited by the chemical industry as well as being used as animal fodder. In recent years the cultivation of citrus fruits has also been developed, particularly in the fertile valleys above the coast.

Cork-oak bark at Santiago do Cacém

Shorthorn cows and cattle egrets

Évora

*I*n 1986, UNESCO declared Évora a World Heritage Site, in recognition of the fabulous collection of architectural gems tightly clustered within this walled city. There are innumerable points of historical interest to detain sightseers as they wander along the cobbled streets that link the city's many paved squares, where students from the university sit strumming guitars or leafing through textbooks. From dusk until midnight, many of the finest buildings are floodlit, making for a romantic evening tour (see page 28).

CONVENTO DOS LÓIOS

The conventual quarters of this 15th-century monastery have been imaginatively converted into a *pousada*. Guests now sleep in the old monastic cells, while two sides of the cloister have been turned into the dining area and the chapter house serves as a lounge. The church of São João Evangelista (St John the Evangelist) adjoins the monastery and is worth seeing for the beautiful *azulejo* tiles which line the nave. They were painted by António de Oliveira Bernardes who

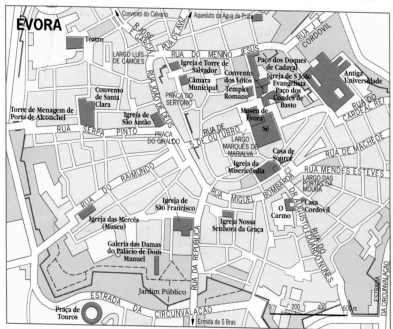

many experts consider to be the finest of all Portuguese tile artists.

Largo Marquês de Marialva. Tel: 066 24051. Open: church 9am–noon, 2–5pm. Admission charge (the same ticket admits to the adjacent Paço dos Duques de Cadaval – see below).

MUSEU DE ÉVORA (Municipal Museum)

This museum, housed in the 17th-century former archbishop's palace, is one of the best in Portugal, renowned for its sculpture (from Roman to modern) and its medieval works of art. The star of the museum is the cathedral altarpiece, 13 panels dating to around 1500, depicting the *Life of the Virgin*.

Largo Conde de Vila Flor. Tel: 066 22604. Open: Tuesday to Sunday 10am–12.30pm, 2–5pm. Closed: Monday.

PAÇO DOS DUQUES DE CADAVAL (Palace of the Dukes of Cadaval)

A short way downhill from the Roman temple is this 14th-century palace topped by a pair of imposing crenellated towers, one of which formed part of the old city walls. Inside is a small art gallery exhibiting rows of stony faced ancestral portraits along with some historic family documents. More interesting and beautiful are the splendid painted ceiling and the pair of 15th-century Flemish bronze commemorative plaques.

Largo Marquês de Marialva. Open: 10am–noon, 2–5pm. Admission charge (the same ticket admits to the Convento dos Lóios – see opposite).

SÃO FRANCISCO

This 15th-century church features on the itinerary of most visitors because of its extraordinary Capela dos Ossos (Chapel

Évora, a town of romantic paved squares and historic buildings

of Bones) decorated with designs made from the bones of 5,000 human skeletons. Skulls grin at you from the walls and the ceiling, while the shrivelled corpses of a man and a child hang at the far end of the chapel. The smell of death seems to linger in the air; an inscription in Portuguese translates as: 'We bones lie here waiting for yours.' Although the macabre chapel revolts many people, it also seems to exercise an irresistible magnetism.

The chapel is approached through the chapter house in which wax images of arms, feet, breasts and other appropriate parts of the anatomy have been placed by way of offerings for people suffering injuries, disease or infertility. At the chapel entrance, braids of human hair have been pinned to the wall; these are placed as votive offerings by young brides-to-be before their weddings.

Rua da República. Tel: 066 24521. Open: Monday to Saturday 8.30am–1pm, 2.30–6pm; Sunday 10–11.30am, 2.30–6pm. Admission charge.

ÉVORA

SÉ (Cathedral)

The façade of the 12th- and 13th-century cathedral looks down on Largo Marquês de Marialva and the city's Roman temple, built a 1,000 years previously. The two huge and sturdy fortress-like towers were added in the 16th century; they are strangely dissimilar since only one of them is topped with turrets.

The intricately sculpted stone statues of the Apostles, guarding the main entrance, are well worth a look. Inside there are three great naves and a soaring vaulted ceiling from which hang some enormous chandeliers. Don't miss the beautiful octagonal dome above the transept or the wooden stalls of the choir, carved in Renaissance style, reached by a staircase at the back.

The same staircase gives access to the cathedral's Museum of Sacred Art, where the ageing custodian in faded uniform might show you photographs of himself in the company of Queen

Sturdy 16th-century towers rising above the façade of Évora's cathedral

Elizabeth II, former US President Ronald Reagan and various other heads of state whose visits to Portugal include the mandatory tour of Évora. The museum houses an extensive collection of bejewelled gold and silver chalices and crucifixes, and some unbelievably ornate ecclesiastical vestments and mitres. The most extraordinary exhibit is an ivory carving of the *Virgin of Paradise,* believed to have been sculpted in the 13th century. The statue opens up to reveal three minutely carved scenes of the *Annunciation,* the *Nativity* and the *Assumption of the Virgin* into heaven.

Adjacent to the cathedral is the 14th-century Gothic cloister of carved granite. A worn and narrow stone staircase at each corner leads up to a terrace which looks down on the cloister and its small enclosed garden; there are also fine views over the town from the crenellated walls of the terrace.

Largo Marquês de Marialva. Tel: 066 26910. Open: daily 9am–7pm. Admission free to the cathedral; admission charge to the choir stalls, cloister and Museum of Religious Art. Open: Tuesday to Sunday 9am–noon, 2–4.30pm.

The cloister of the Antiga Universidade, Évora's 16th-century university

Intriguing views in Évora

TEMPLO ROMANO (Roman Temple)

Commonly known as the 'Temple of Diana', this is the most outstanding Roman monument in Portugal. Built in the 2nd century AD, the Corinthian-style temple of marble plinths and granite columns stands in the middle of Largo de Marquês de Marialva in the shadow of the grey, Gothic cathedral. Over the centuries the temple has been partly dismantled and used as a convenient source of building material for others of the city's monuments. Six columns, however, remain perfectly intact; its usefulness as a medieval market-place and, until 1870, as the city's municipal abattoir, probably prevented its total destruction.

Largo Marquês de Marialva. Open: all day. Free.

Location: Évora is on the N18, 46km from Estremoz. Tourist office: Praça do Giraldo. Tel: 066 22671. Open: Monday to Friday 9am–7pm, weekends 9am–12.30pm, 2–7pm.

ÉVORA MONTE

The castle and the tiny village of Évora Monte, sitting atop a steep hill, command one of the most spectacular panoramas in the Upper Alentejo. Expansive 360-degree views take in the two cities and boundless plains dotted with white villages. For this alone, an energetic scramble or an engine-straining 1.5km drive to the top is well rewarded.

Évora Monte is where the peace treaty was signed in 1834 ending the so-called 'War of the Two Brothers', the civil war fought between Pedro IV and his brother Miguel. This was one of the most important events in recent Portuguese history and that may be why the authorities have seen fit to rebuild the once derelict castle keep, creating a four-storey reconstruction of the medieval original in painted cement. From a distance it looks like a giant sandcastle with four large circular towers. Fortunately, this is not an experiment that has been repeated anywhere else in the Alentejo; it proves only that it is possible to ruin a good ruin.

Inside is a rather strange collection of exhibits including reconstructed looms illustrating the traditional carpet-weaving industry of the region. More appropriately, there are displays of historical documentation explaining how the original castle was captured from the

Évora Monte – reconstruction of the medieval castle in painted concrete

Moors in the 12th century and how an earthquake destroyed it in 1531, following which it was rebuilt with the thick-set towers reproduced so incongruously in the late 20th century. However, the crumbling ramparts, the old town gate, the church and the one-street village retain some of Évora Monte's ambience.

Évora Monte Castle, Rua da Convenção. Tel: 068 95277. Open: daily 9am–noon, 2–5pm, except Tuesday. Free.

Location: Évora Monte is signposted off the N18 halfway between Évora and Estremoz.

MARVÃO

'You have Portugal at your feet and, in opening your arms, Spain', wrote the Portuguese poet, José Amaro, of Marvão. It is apparent, from a long way away, why Marvão became one of the most strategic fortified positions on Portugal's eastern flank. Situated in a raw and remote area, high up on one of the highest peaks of the São Mamede ridge which forms a natural border with Spain, this medieval town has dominating views over Spain to the east and over Portugal's highest mountain range, the Serra da Estrela, to the north. All around are cliffs sheer enough to make the town virtually unassailable.

A narrow and tortuous road leads up to the craggy summit, where Marvão perches. Within the walls there is only a handful of tightly clustered houses, mainly because the town never had any real function, other than as a garrison. A walk round the walls is a delightful way to spend half an hour, as is a stroll through the steep, winding, cobbled streets. To reach the austere and forbidding 13th-century castle keep, you

Commemorative plaque and royal crown embellishing a building in Évora Monte

will have to pass through several gates in the otherwise impenetrable walls and venture on to a parapet along the rock overhang.

Marvão's history is peppered with sieges and battles: it was a Moorish stronghold until finally being taken by the Christian King Afonso I in the 12th century. Over the subsequent centuries it was on the front line of Portugal's struggle to win and maintain independence from Spain. From 1640 to 1660, after the enemy from the east had been driven out and João IV set on the throne, Marvão was relentlessly attacked by Spain in a vain attempt to reconquer Portugal. Napoleon's forces took the town at the start of the Peninsula War but were driven out in 1808.

Location: Marvão is signposted off the N246, 24km north of Portalegre.

Precipitous streets in Mértola

MÉRTOLA

Mértola stands at the highest navigable point on the Rio Guadiana, the river that divides Portugal from Spain for 100km or so, before it curves inland leaving a rocky ridge of mountains to take over as the natural border. Phoenicians and Carthaginians sailed up as far as Mértola to trade and the Romans established a permanent base there.

The remains of a Roman wharf can still be seen down by the waterside. For defensive reasons, the main part of the town is high above, on a hillside overlooking the river gorge and the confluence of the Oeiras tributary with the Guadiana.

The Moors left a much greater impact on the town. In the middle of Mértola is a domed mosque, one of only two known to have survived the zealous Christian assaults on infidel places of worship that took place after the expulsion of the Moors (the other is at Serpa). Follow signs to the 'Mesquita' which is now the parish church; statues of Christ and the Virgin look out across 12 Moorish columns but the faithful still face east towards Mecca just as their Muslim predecessors did. The low square crenellated building has been given a Renaissance doorway and a bell tower, but is nevertheless dis-orientatingly at odds with any other church in Portugal.

The castle walls are Moorish too, built on Roman foundations. Within them, crowning the town, is a 13th-century keep. On display inside are pieces of carved stone from the Roman, Visigothic, Moorish and Christian eras, each of which left an influence on the castle. Down the hill, in the centre of town, is the small Museu Municipal where more inscribed stones are exhibited, along with Moorish pottery, human bones and the remains of some curious dolls.

Bird-watchers are frequently to be found in Mértola, observing the storks; these have claimed the highest roof-tops as nesting points, from where they glide over the gorge below. A flock of rare black vultures is also sometimes to be seen flapping over the town in search of the carrion that is left out for them.

There is nobody in permanent attendance at either the mosque or the castle, but ask for Senhora Maria or Senhor Manuel, the couple who keep the keys. Free, but a gratuity is expected for the caretakers.

The Museu Municipal (tel: 084 62125), is

*open daily 10am–1pm, 2.30–5pm,
except Saturday, Sunday and public
holidays.*

*Location: Mértola is on the N122, 50km
south of Beja.*

MIRÓBRIGA

Miróbriga is one of Portugal's most
outstanding archaeological sites. A
settlement is thought to have been
founded here by Celtic migrants in
the 4th century BC. From the pottery
and coins of this era found on the site,
it is evident that it became an
important centre of trade, with links
across southern Spain. Even so, it is
the remains of the 1st-century AD
Roman city which provide the most
palpable sense of the past. It is well
worth wandering around the site for
half an hour to get acclimatised
before viewing the excavations in
detail.

A large part of this great Roman city
remains unexcavated and lies under the
bumpy, pitted green hills of the site, but
the 25,000-capacity amphitheatre, where
citizens would have watched horse-
racing, gives a clue to its full dimensions.
So, too, does the bathhouse, which is in
a much better state of repair; plumbing
experts can marvel at the water heating
system and the pipes which filled the
cold, tepid and hot baths. At the highest
point on the site are the relics of temples
to Venus and Aesculapius. Many of the
archaeological finds from Miróbriga are
now in Santiago do Cacém's Museu
Municipal.

*Location: off the N120 road, signposted to
Lisbon, about 1km north of Santiago do
Cacém. Open: daily 9am–noon,
12.45–6.45pm, except Sunday, Monday
and public holidays. Admission charge.*

Roman temple ruins at Miróbriga, an
outstanding archaeological site

MONSARAZ

Like many in the chain of fortified hilltops that run along Portugal's eastern border with Spain, Monsaraz huddles entirely within its impregnable walls. So compact is this village, high above the Guadiana river and overlooking Spain, that even the main street is too narrow for a car. This adds to the distinctly medieval ambience which still pervades the place: mangy dogs lollop about while black-clad women sit behind dark windows, protected by wrought-iron grilles, in the cool of their low tumbledown cottages.

Because of its strategic position, Monsaraz was the site of a prehistoric settlement, then a Roman, Visigothic and Moorish village before being taken from the Moors in 1167. It was heavily fortified in the 14th century by King Dinis, when the formidable ramparts, square towers and castle were built. In front of the two-storey pentagonal keep is a square where bullfights are held on

Views from the ramparts in the fortified village of Monsaraz

feast days, while villagers sit cheering from the surrounding stone walls.

The view from the parapets is stunning; the plains of the Alentejo stretch out endlessly towards the coast, whose outline just becomes visible on

Monsaraz – the Igreja Matriz

the horizon when it is exceptionally clear. The rocky, meandering Guadiana river, to the east, provides a dramatic contrast, while Spain extends beyond like a crumpled rug.

There are several points of interest on Rua Direita, the cobbled main street, which is lined with houses emblazoned with the coats of arms of wealthy 16th- and 17th-century families. Do not miss the Paços do Concelho Tribunal Building; this has a 15th-century fresco illustrating a judge being tempted by an impish, bribe-offering devil while simultaneously being drawn to the outstretched arms and majestic justice of Christ. An elaborately carved marble tomb in the Igreja Matriz (Parish Church) is worth a look.

Location: Monsaraz is on the N319, 7km off the N256, between Évora and Mourão.

MOURA

Moura means a 'Moorish Maiden' and the name refers to the legendary Salúquia, the daughter of a Moorish nobleman from Al-Manija (as the town was then called). Her marriage came to grief when her bridegroom and his entourage were attacked and killed by a band of Christians on their way to the wedding ceremony.

The Christians then donned the nuptial clothes of their victims convincingly enough for the city's drawbridge to be lowered for them. By this means they were able to capture the town and Salúquia; the Moura, threw herself from the castle tower in grief. The story is unusual among Portuguese folk legends in that it casts the Christians in the role of villains.

More prosaic history books have it that Moura first fell to the Christians in 1165, and that it subsequently changed

hands several times. Today it is a fairly busy agricultural town with a lively Mouraria (Moorish quarter) of cobbled streets and low houses pierced by arches and ornamented with rounded, tile-topped chimneys. The castle is now a ruin, having been blown up during the Spanish War of Succession, although the keep, a tower and parts of the wall are still there.

Monumental fountain in Moura

The 13th-century Convento do Carmo, the first Carmelite convent in Portugal, is worth a visit to see the frescoed ceiling in the chancel, which was rebuilt in 1725. The Gothic Igreja do São João church is also interesting; notice the columns of smooth-carved marble supporting the pulpit, and the 17th-century *azulejo* tiles in a side chapel at the south end of the church.

Location: Moura is 35km northeast of Serpa at the hub of seven roads radiating out across east-central Alentejo.

MOURÃO

This remote little town, on the east side of the Guadiana river, just 7km from the Spanish border, is another in the string of fortified strongholds running down the country's eastern flank. Its name relates directly to a Moorish past but, curiously, the original town was located below the present site, down towards the river. Some say that river-borne disease drove the population uphill; others that it was the castle's indefensible position.

The neglected ruins of what is known as the Vila Velha (Old Town) are worth visiting for a ramble round the ramparts and the three towers, all that is left of the ancient castle.

Location: Mourão is on the N256, 7km west of the frontier post at São Leonardo and 20km east of Reguengos de Monsaraz.

PORTALEGRE

Allow plenty of time to see Portalegre, the capital of the Upper Alentejo, located near the northern extremity of the province. This small but bustling city, in the foothills of the Serra de São Mamede mountain range, is surrounded by green, fecund countryside which contrasts sharply with the burnt plains and rugged hills further south. King Dinis fortified the town in 1290 because of its proximity to the Spanish border. In 1704 it fell briefly to the Spanish during the Spanish War of Succession then, during the Peninsular War, it was held by Napoleon's troops. Little of the castle or city walls survive today.

A prominent feature of Portalegre's history is its position as a centre for wool and silk weaving; the resulting prosperity provided for many of the city's most interesting sights.

Manufactura de Tapeçarias (Tapestry Factory)

This was established in 1947, building

The fortified stronghold of Mourão, a frontier town on the Spanish border

on the town's centuries-old weaving tradition, and has become one of the foremost centres in Europe for tapestry weaving. The workshop is housed in a 17th-century former Jesuit seminary, where visitors can follow the extraordinary process, on a 45-minute guided tour.

No two tapestries are alike, and each is specially commissioned by the client; many of them are copies of paintings, or even photographs. The first stage is to make a transparency of the work, which is then produced in the most unbelievably intricate detail on paper, matching colours to a selection of nearly 8,000 different shades of wool. These are then minutely stitched to create a wonderfully tactile version of the original.

Tel: 045 33024. Open: Monday to Friday, except public holidays; tours at 10am and 4pm. Admission charge.

The Tapestry Factory, Portalegre

Museu Municipal

This small museum, housed in the 18th-century former diocesan seminary just behind the cathedral, contains a rather motley but occasionally interesting group of collections: snuffboxes, Chinese porcelain and ivory carvings, for example. Among the religious art is a dazzling array of gold and silver chalices and crucifixes, some elaborate vestments, a beautiful 17th-century tabernacle carved in ivory and an extensive collection of paintings, carvings, prints and trinkets – all of them images of Santo António, the patron saint of travellers.

Praça do Município, Câmara Municipal. Tel: 045 21616. Open: Monday and Wednesday to Friday 9.30am–12.30pm, 2–6pm; Saturday 3–6.30pm. Closed: Sunday and Tuesday. Admission charge.

Sé (Cathedral)

The huge cathedral is never out of sight, its pinnacles towering above the city. It was begun in the 16th century in Renaissance style, while the façade, of wrought-iron balconies and marble pillars, was added in the 18th century. The cavernous, triple-naved interior can be refreshingly cool on a summer's day; don't miss the 18th-century *azulejo* tiles in the sacristy, illustrating the *Flight into Egypt,* or the fine paintings and altarpieces to be found in several of the side chapels.

Open: daily. Free.

Location: Portalegre is on the N359, 57km north of Estremoz and 81km northeast of Elvas. Tourist office: 25 Estrada da Santa. Tel: 045 21815.

FAMILY LIFE

In Portugal, among both rich and poor, the family unit is exceptionally important and everyone feels a strong sense of kinship and loyalty towards it. Being a Roman Catholic country, families are often large and embrace several generations. It is common for young children to be cared for by grandparents or by their older brothers and sisters. This is particularly true of rural areas because it enables both parents to work on the land.

The poverty of rural life means that children tend to live at home until they are married; even then, it is not uncommon for a newly married couple to move in with one set of parents.

In a peasant economy, shortage of land forces many parents to work especially hard in order to save and give a head start to their children. Working abroad, sometimes for several years, is one way of making vital extra money and most families possess at least one

member who is *la fora* ('out there').

In the houses of the Algarve and the Alentejo, the kitchen is very much the centre of family. The domestic economy is organised around the seasons and in such a way that nothing is wasted. If a pig is killed everybody participates and a use is found for every part of the animal.

Outside of the kitchen there is not much division of labour by gender; socially, however, the local bar tends to be a male preserve while women will often be seen crocheting in groups outside their houses or in the town square. Women live longer than men, which explains the plenitude of old ladies dressed in black, the conventions of mourning still being strictly observed.

Although family life is central to Catholic Portugal, men and women still tend to lead separate social lives

Enchanting and colourful Porto Covo,
lovingly tended by its inhabitants

PORTO COVO DA BANDEIRA

This is an enchanting little seaside
village, on the Atlantic coast, that has
retained its character in a way which
would be quite impossible if it were on
the Algarve. The sea tends to be a few
degrees cooler than on the south coast
and a strong wind can blow from the
north at any time of year. Despite this,
Porto Covo satisfies the yearnings of
people looking for a quiet and
characterful fishing port.

The low, Moorish-influenced houses
are uniformly whitewashed and have
red-tiled roofs and sea-blue borders
round their doors and windows. If you
wind your way through the leafy main

THE HERMIT OF PORTO COVO

An oft-repeated legend in Porto Covo
tells of a hermit who lived on the
offshore island and was much
revered for this holiness. Pirates
attacked the island, killed the hermit
and made a fire of his few
possessions, which included a
carved wooden image of the Virgin.
When fishermen subsequently sifted
through the ashes, they found the
Madonna unscathed. They took it to
the mainland and built a chapel to
Nossa Senhora da Queimada (Our
Lady of the Burning), which
subsequently became a pilgrimage
destination.

square and along spotlessly clean
cobbled streets, you will come down to
the seafront with its handful of shops
and beach bars; here you can eat
barbecued fish or octopus, fresh off the
gaily painted wooden boats which put to
sea from the port.

The coastline is splintered in both
directions into cliffs, secluded coves and
inlets, fine sandy beaches and rocky
outcrops. Just visible to the south, about
a 1km out to sea, is an island known as
Ilha do Pessegueiro ('Peach Tree
Island').

There's usually a fisherman on the
beach willing to take people across for a
negotiated fee but you will not find fruit
trees of any description there – the island
is entirely barren. However, there is a
small ruined fortress and harbour to be
explored as you play at being Robinson
Crusoe. The fortress was built in the
17th century as a base for pre-emptive
strikes against the pirates who lurked
offshore, waiting to attack the coastal
villages of the Alentejo. It was badly
damaged in the same earthquake of 1755
that razed Lisbon to the ground, and
now survives only as a romantic ruin.
Location: Porto Covo is 6km off the N120
which leads southwards from Sines to the
Algarve.

REGUENGOS DE MONSARAZ

Reguengos de Monsaraz is a small
agricultural centre on the Alentejo
plains, surrounded by huge tracts of cork
oak forest, olive groves, sunflower fields
and vineyards. The town was originally
founded by people from Monsaraz, the
nearby fortress (see page 110), so that
they could grow food. The name
Reguengos indicates that the land once
belonged to the crown.

As Reguengos de Monsaraz is one of

The coastline round Porto Covo varies from
windblown dunes to secluded coves

the most festive towns in Portugal, a visit
may well coincide with a *feira* (fair) or
festa (festival). There are parish fairs
(Feiras da Freguesia de Reguengos de
Monsaraz) in January, May and August;
these are the best times to view the local
hand-painted pottery, woven carpets
and other handicrafts. There are
religious festivals, with fireworks and
processions, for the festivals of São
Marcos in late April, Santo António in
June and Nosso Senhor Jesus dos Passos
in September.

Since the mid-1980s, full-bodied red
wines from Reguengos have achieved
widespread acclaim, and are available in
specialist wine shops around Europe.
You can visit the Cooperativa Agricola
de Reguengos de Monsaraz to taste the
wines or stock up.
Cooperativa Agricola de Reguengos de
Monsaraz, 5 Rua Conde de Monsaraz.
Tel: 066 51541. Open: by prior appoint-
ment. Free.

Location: Reguengos de Monsaraz is on the
N256, 35km southeast of Évora and 15km
west of Monsaraz.

FESTIVE LIFE

Portugal is a Catholic country and, as well as celebrating all the major feasts in the church calendar, it has numerous traditional festivals, called *romarias,* in honour of locally revered saints. The patron saint acts as a focus of unity for the community and celebrations held around the time of the saint's feast day are often extravagant events involving costumed processions, firework displays and, almost always, a fair. *Romarias* are less common in the south, which is much less devout than the north, but it is always worth checking to see if your stay coincides with a local festival.

Many festivals have pagan dimensions and celebrate the arrival of the spring, including the festival at Loulé, known as the Battle of the Flowers, which welcomes the blossoming of the almond. Summer festivals offer you the best chance of witnessing traditional country dancing and other vestiges of local folklore.

Country fairs *(feiras)* are also events to look out for. As well as the many weekly fairs, or markets, there are several large annual events, such as the September livestock fair at Moura and the May fair at Vila Viçosa. These are enormously lively and enjoyable occasions, with a vast range of country products on sale, ranging from pots and blankets to home-made food.

National holidays include Carnaval, marking the beginning of Lent, which is nowhere near as riotous as its Brazilian counterpart but can still be a noisy and inebriated event, and Portugal Day, which celebrates the 16th-century poet Camões with festivities and recitations from his epic poem, *Os Lusíadas (The Lusiads).*

Dancers and musicians exhibit their skills at one of southern Portugal's regular folk festivals

Festival lights

SERPA

Serpa stands slightly elevated from the fertile plains of the Alentejo on the first folds of the mountains that form Portugal's eastern border. Low-built whitewashed houses, with red-tiled roofs, line the cobbled streets, while the balconies of grander homes overlook white-paved squares. These days the town is a fairly important agricultural hub although, if you turn up on a summer's afternoon, you might be forgiven for suspecting that a Pied Piper had led away the entire population, save the occasional old man whiling away the hours in the shade. Later in the day, when the cottage windows are unshuttered and the cafés open, Serpa can be the place to feel the soul of the Alentejo embodied. You are also likely to encounter groups of troubadours in traditional dress who wander the ancient streets wailing mournful songs; these have their roots in Moorish times and have been handed down over countless generations.

Houses in the old part of the town are dwarfed by remains of the rambling and ruinous fortress, by some formidably sturdy and crenellated stretches of the city wall and by a high slender aqueduct. The castle and fortifications were built by King Dinis after the Moors were finally driven out in 1232; most of the damage they sustained occurred nearly 500 years later, during the Spanish War of Succession, when the town was blown up in a series of massive explosions ordered by the Spanish Duke of Ossuña.

From next to the grey Gothic parish church, the unmistakable Igreja Matriz, a steep stone staircase climbs up on to the walls from where the whole town,

Serpa's city wall, built in 1232 after the final expulsion of the Moors

and its situation on the plains, can be put into glorious perspective. The tiny Museu de Serpa, just next to the entrance to the castle only has one notable exhibit: a life-size and highly realistic tableau of the *Last Supper*.
Museu de Serpa. Open: daily 9am–12.30pm, 4–7.30pm in summer; 9am–12.30pm, 4–5.30pm in winter. Free.

Nearby
About 2km out of town, next to Serpa's modern *pousada* (which enjoys glorious views over the plains) is a small former mosque, now called the Capela de São Gens. This is one of only two known mosques surviving in Portugal, the other one being at Mértola. It is a quintessentially Moorish building of low domes, archways and finials, all washed glaringly white to reflect the sun and leave the interior cool.
Capela de São Gens, Largo do Salvador. Take the E52 eastwards out of town, and turn right following the sign to the pousada. Open: daily 9am–7pm. Free.

Location: Serpa is 28km southeast of Beja. Tourist office: Praça da República. Tel: 084 53727.

SINES
The birthplace of Vasco da Gama, discoverer of the sea route to India, is a changed place these days. Until about 20 years ago the richly characterful old town, with its castle and sandy beach stretching down to the headland of Cabo de Sines, was one of the most attractive fishing ports on the Alentejo coast. Today the town is again world famous in maritime circles, but this time on account of the deepwater harbour built to accommodate the huge oil tankers

Statue of Vasco da Gama in Sines, the town of his birth

that dock here to disgorge their hundreds of thousands of tonnes of crude oil at the town's colossal refinery.

Tar defiles the beach and the whiff of chemicals lingers in the air, making Sines a poor choice of place to stay; but it is worth a stop, particularly for devotees of Portugal's great seafaring history. Despite the refinery, the old town still retains much of its charm and you can visit the castle, widely held to be the birthplace of Vasco da Gama. A colourful religious festival takes place during the first fortnight in August, reaching a climax on 15 August, the Feast of the Assumption.
Sines Castle. Tel: 069 862188. Open: daily 9am–12.30pm, 2–5.30pm. Admission charge.

Location: Sines lies 20km southwest of Santiago de Cacém.

TRÓIA PENINSULA

The Tróia Peninsula is a long narrow spit jutting 20km out of the northwest corner of the Alentejo, towards the great industrial metropolis of Setúbal. To one side of this sandy, marshy promontory is the lake-like estuary of the Rio Sado, which the peninsula almost encloses; on the other is the Atlantic.

The peninsula is lined with hotels and is a popular holiday resort, as well as a day-trip destination for the people of Lisbon and Setúbal. Beaches on the Sado estuary side of the promontory tend to be more crowded because the water is calmer, and usually a couple of degrees warmer. However, dedicated sea bathers should make for the western side, only a few hundred metres away, where great Atlantic rollers frequently crash on to the sand.

At the furthermost tip of Tróia is the Torralta Tourist Development, a huge, high-rise complex with hotels, restaurants, a golf-course and every kind of watersports facility. The beach is excellent, but it does get very crowded in the high season.

Cetóbriga

This is an interesting semi-excavated Roman site on the Sado estuary side of the peninsula. It was founded in the 1st century AD and grew into one of the most important fishing and fish-processing towns in the Roman Empire. Archaeologists believe that a tidal wave, caused by an earthquake, was responsible for its destruction in the 5th century AD. However, the fish-processing tradition of the area has endured to the present day; in Setúbal, just across the water, this is a massive industry.

Ancient docks and fish-processing equipment have been unearthed at Cetóbriga and these can be viewed, along with a bathhouse, gymnasium, chapel and fragments of fresco.
Cetóbriga is on the left bank of the Rio Sado, facing Setúbal. Tel: 065 44151. Open: Tuesday to Sunday, 9am–noon, 2–7pm. Free.

Reserva Natural do Estuario do Sado (The Sado Estuary Nature Reserve)

The reserve includes most of the land bordering on the estuary, as well as the base of the Tróia Peninsula. The habitat consists of marshland and mudflats,

The Sado Estuary Nature Reserve

bordered by rolling banks of sand dune. The reserve is home to cranes, storks, egrets, all kinds of wildfowl and countless species of migratory birds. Dolphins and otters are also occasionally spotted in the estuary. It is easily accessible by roads leading off the E52 north from Alcácer do Sal, and is best explored on foot, preferably armed with a pair of binoculars.

Location: the Tróia Peninsula is on the N253 west of Alcácer do Sal.

VIANA DO ALENTEJO

By-passed by most tourists, because it is not served by any main roads, this secretive little town hides behind its crenellated walls. It has a small atmospheric castle and one of the most unusual and interesting churches in the Alentejo.

The castle could be straight out of a picture book. You can walk round the rectangular ramparts and battlements,

The battlemented church of Viana do Alentejo

linking four cylindrical towers, for views of the town and the plains beyond. Within the walls are some well-tended gardens with lawns and privet hedges.

The Church of Nossa Senhora da Assunção is also fortified with crenellations, with turrets in place of bell towers, so that, from a distance, church and castle appear to merge together into a single entity. Beneath the battlements of the façade, however, is a fine Manueline doorway. The interior is an unusual mixture of Romanesque with Manueline embellishments. The roof is supported by octagonal carved stone pillars. All the way round the base of the nave is a fringe of superb 17th-century _azulejo_ tiles. Don't miss the rather splendid Crucifix in the chancel.
Location: Viana do Alentejo is 29km southwest of Évora.

The sandy Rio Mira estuary

VILA NOVA DE MILFONTES

Vila Nova de Milfontes is the Alentejo's
busiest seaside holiday resort. Although
its scale pales in comparison to the
mammoth developments of the Algarve,
this quaint and attractive old fishing port
is very fashionable and hugely popular
with people from Lisbon and the
Alentejo hinterland. Standing on the
sandy north bank of the wide estuary of
the Rio Mira, the resort has the
advantage of long stretches of superb
beach and a choice of either the Atlantic
or the warmer, calmer estuary for
swimming and watersports.

Although surrounded by modern
hotels, the old town still oozes character.
The maze of medieval cobbled streets is
sprinkled with restaurants serving
mouthwateringly fresh fish and seafood.
The 16th-century fort, which is now a
hotel and not open to the public, has a
fascinating history dating back to the

times when Milfontes was in constant
danger from piracy. Arab pirates would
lurk off the coast waiting to plunder the
town or kidnap its inhabitants, to be
held for ransom or sold as slaves back in
North Africa. King João's answer to the
defence of Milfontes was to declare the
town a safe haven for all Portuguese
fugitives evading the law; in return, they
had to agree to stay in the town and
defend the castle whenever it came
under attack.
*Location: Vila Nova de Milfontes is 41km
south of Sines.*

VILA VIÇOSA

This royal city was once the seat of the
Dukes of Bragança, the family that
provided Portugal with its monarchs
from 1640 until the proclamation of the
republic in 1910. The city's regal
buildings provide a very striking contrast
to the medieval fortified hilltops and
Moorish-influenced architecture that
characterises most of the Alentejo. Vila

Window on the world, Vila Nova

Viçosa (literally 'Shaded Town') is dominated by the magnificent three-storey Paça Ducal (Ducal Palace). This overlooks an expansive marble-paved square, with its statue of João IV, the first of the Bragança kings. Streets lined with orange trees lead to the outlying plains which were once covered with great tracts of prime hunting forest; this is usually offered as the reason why the Bragança dukes chose the town as their principal residence. Nowadays, Vila Viçosa is essentially a museum town, as evidenced by the rows of tour coaches parked in the square and the packs of escorted groups filing through the palace.

Paço Ducal (Ducal Palace)

The 110m-long white marble façade of the palace forms one side of the main square. Visitors waiting at the entrance for their guided tour will first see a series of huge paintings that depict some of Portugal's greatest military triumphs. The palace is now entirely a museum filled with fine art, porcelain, tapestries and other treasures of the royal era.

The halls of the main wing are hung with vast tapestries glorifying the 15th-century Age of Discovery, when Portugal was at the forefront of exploration in Asia and the Americas. There are also some superb 17th-century *azulejo* tiles on the walls, while the ceilings are painted with biblical and mythological scenes, such as the story of *David and Goliath* and the adventures of *Perseus in the Underworld*. From the great stone window frames you can look out over the immaculately tended gardens, where peacocks strut amid the topiary.

In the adjacent transverse wing are the royal apartments, last used by King Carlos I, the penultimate Portuguese

The royal city of Vila Viçosa

monarch, who left Vila Viçosa for Lisbon on 1 February, 1908, along with his eldest son, the heir to the throne. They were both assassinated along the route. The younger son, Manuel II, reigned briefly before being forced into exile in England in 1910; there he died in 1932, leaving all his wealth, including the treasures of Vila Viçosa, to the Portuguese nation.

Two other points of interest in the palace are the collection of royal carriages and the kitchens; here enormous gleaming copper cauldrons and huge roasting spits evoke the era of royal hunting and feasting.

Paça Ducal. Tel: 068 98659. Open: daily 9.30am–1pm, 2–6pm, except Sunday, Monday and public holidays. Admission charge.

Location: Vila Viçosa is on the N255, 18km southeast of Estremoz. Tourist office: Praça da República. Tel: 068 881101.

WILDLIFE

Southern Portugal has a varied wildlife, though some animals are under threat. The wolf *(lobo)* could still be found in southern Portugal up until 20 years ago. Both the badger *(texugo)* and the fox *(raposo)* are increasingly rare. Only slightly more common is the civet cat *(gato-de-Algália)* regarded as a threat to poultry and shot on sight. The rabbit *(coelho)* is hunted for its meat and is more plentiful than the hare *(lebre),* especially in the Barrocal region of the Algarve.

The only poisonous snake in the south is the snub-nosed viper, found in the mountains. The one you are most likely to see is the horseshoe snake, which is dark with yellow spots and a mark on its neck that explains its name. There are several types of lizard including salamanders, chameleons, geckos and the European green lizard.

Even greater variety can be found in the region's bird life, since Portugal is on the main route for migrating birds. There are nature reserves between the Guadiana river and Castro Marim, on the dunes between Faro and Olhão and on the Tróia Peninsula in the Alentejo. Golden eagles are now very rare but red kites and kestrels are not unusual. Startling, but common, is the sight of the brightly coloured hoopoe.

Egrets can be found, with many other waders, at the mouth of the Guadiana river and cattle egrets can be seen in the Alentejo. The eastern Alentejo is home to flocks of azure-winged magpies. Also quite common in the south is the white stork *(cegonha)* which builds its great nest on church bell towers or other high and isolated buildings.

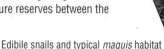

Edibile snails and typical *maquis* habitat

Cattle egret (*Bubulcus ibis*)
in the Alentejo

The azure-winged magpie
(*Cyanopica cyanus*)

The ocellated lizard

Getting Away From it All

*T*he whole of the Alentejo region, with its sparsely populated hilltop villages and endless horizons, will appeal to the traveller in search of an escape from the crowds. The same cannot be said of the Algarve, with its villa developments and leisure complexes, but there is still far more to this region than a long beach backed by a furious highway. Of course one way to get away from it all is to visit southern Portugal out of season – especially in the spring when you will be able to enjoy the superb wild flowers as well as the absence of other visitors. Other than that, there are plenty of opportunities to find peace, adventure or relative solitude on those days that you don't want to spend on a busy beach.

The ochre-coloured cliffs of Praia da Rocha

Adventure excursions

One way to explore the backroads and mountains of the Algarve is by joining an organised excursion, usually billed as a 'safari', travelling in a four-wheel drive vehicle to explore the roughest terrain of the *serra* – the mountainous region separating the Algarve from the Alentejo. Several companies advertise in the main coastal resorts and out of Évora – ask for information at local tourist offices – and many offer big-game fishing trips, yacht charter or balloon flights as well. If you are interested, check their itineraries, and – most important – the insurance cover they offer. Some car rental companies offer four-wheel drive jeeps if you want to make the trip independently. To see how the professionals do it, watching an off-road rally offers the excitement of racing in remote countryside: the largest is the annual Transalgarve in March. If the roar of a straining jeep engine is not your idea of an escape, consider a journey on horseback instead. Look for signs to 'Centro Hípico'.

Beaches

Despite the popularity if the big names such as Albufeira, Praia da Rocha or Quarteira, substantial parts of the Algarve coast remain undeveloped. Some believe it may only be a matter of time before this situation changes, despite the introduction of new planning restrictions by the Portuguese government. Even so, west from Lagos, round Cabo de São Vicente (Cape St Vincent), and north as far as Sines, and again east of Faro, you can still find almost empty beaches, while only a few kilometres inland from these beaches you will discover peaceful, often unspoilt, landscapes.

The least developed beaches are those that stretch north from Cabo de São Vicente. Far from the larger towns and holiday resorts, and sometimes fairly inaccessible, this coast faces the full force of the Atlantic, making it colder and breezier than those around the headland to the south. Beaches such as Praia do Castelejo, Bordeira and Monte Clérigo offer magnificent stretches of windswept sand, backed by deep, wind-formed dunes. The surf is impressive but be careful of strong currents. There are few facilities here, but most of the

Waiting for the shark to bite

beaches have one or two cafés and the nearby villages have accommodation.

On the Alentejo coast, Vila Nova de Milfontes is popular with Lisboners as well as tourists, but halfway between Milfontes and Sines – a place to get away from – the little village of Porto Covo has its own Praia de Conches and lies near the small Ilha do Pessegueiro which you can visit with the help of a local boatman.

The Alvor estuary near Portimão – now declared a nature reserve

Islands

Many of the most remote beaches along the southern coast lie on offshore islands or along the sandbars that stretch for up to 12km in length all along the balmy *sotavento* (leeward) coast east of Faro. Some, especially those served by regular ferries, can get quite busy in high season, while with others the only way to get there is to persuade a local fisherman to take you across (and pick you up again) by boat. Ilha de Tavira is a long sandy bar which can get crowded; quieter is Barril, which you can reach from Pedras de El Rei. Both have long sandy beaches with warm water and can be reached by ferry. The Ilha de Faro can be reached by car along the causeway beyond the airport (signposted Praia de Faro), or by ferry from the harbour, but it gets very busy in high season.

The islands off the port of Olhão can be reached by regular ferry in summer; the Ilha da Armona is the nearer, while the Ilha da Culatra, on which stands Faro's lighthouse, or *farol*, is generally quieter.

Boat trips

Instead of driving inland from the crowded beaches of the Algarve, try heading in the opposite direction – out to sea. There is a wide variety of trips on offer all along the southern coast, from a gentle ride up the Guadiana river from Vila Real de Santo António to a deep-sea shark-fishing trip, strictly for those with a strong constitution.

Fishing boats leave from many of the larger fishing ports, including Portimão and Vilamoura. Don't forget that the sun can be even fiercer out at sea than on the beach, while the wind can be more biting; sunblock and a sweater is a good combination.

A boat trip is also the best way to see the fascinating caves and grottoes formed along the *barlavento* (windward) section of the Algarve coast between Albufeira and Lagos. Trips depart from Benagil for the Carvoeiro section, from Lagos or Praia Dona Ana for Ponta da Piedade, from Albufeira west to the Gruta do Xorino (which can also be reached on foot) and from Armação de Pêra for the Gruta do Pontal.

Mountain villages and lakes

It is not just the Alentejo which has remote mountain villages – though few in the Algarve have such dramatic approaches as those to Evoramonte and Monsaraz. Few tourists take time to explore the villages of the mountainous *serra* region, except perhaps for the popular and spectacular drive through the Serra de Monchique to Caldas and Fóia. The villages of the central and eastern Algarve, in particular, are little-known and can present challenging driving, but it can be particularly rewarding to visit a remote chapel or shop at a small market which few others reach.

In the northeast, the N124 leads through one of the most rural parts of the region, near ancient villages such as Vaqueiros, Gilões and Martim Longo, all with fascinating churches, while the N507 follows the banks of the meandering Guadiana river from Alcoutim through tiny hamlets such as Alamo and Foz de Odeleite.

Touring with a purpose, perhaps in search of *azulejos* or a particular market or festival, can take you deep into the back-country of the *serra;* to remote villages such as Cachopo, an ancient place of pilgrimage which centres on its church of Santo Estevão: festivals take

place on the second Sunday in August
and 26 December and the pilgrimage of
Santo Estevão takes place on 20 and 21
September. From Cachopo the N124
continues southwest to Barranco do
Velha, by way of Vales and Feiteira, a
route that offers some great views.

Inland lakes and reservoirs, usually
named after their dams *(barragem)* are
also popular destinations for bird-
watchers, windsurfers and picnickers
alike. The largest in the Algarve is the
Barragem da Bravura, 15km north of
Lagos in the foothills of the Serra de
Espinhaço de Cão; for views of the water
head west from Monchique on the N267
to Aljezur, passing through unspoilt
countryside to the west coast via the
village of Marmelete. Further east, on

The centuries-old spa at Caldas de
Monchique – set in an area famed for
luxuriant woodland and flowers

the N124 from Silves to São Bartolomeu
de Messines, is the turning for the
Barragem de Arade.

There are many more reservoirs in
the Alentejo, though the water level
drops in summer, so don't expect them
always to be as extensive as they appear
on a map. One of the most attractive is
the small Barragem de Tapada Grande
on the N265, which crosses the Serra de
Mértola and Serra de Serpa. Another is
the Barragem de Santa Clara (also called
the Barragem de Marcello Caetano)
reached from the Algarve by heading
north from Monchique on the N266.

Parks and gardens

Évora has its Jardim Publico, complete with bandstand and elegant palace ruins, and the Ducal Palace at Vila Viçosa has its elegant topiary but, on the whole, green parks and ornamental gardens are rare in southern Portugal. Another one worth searching out, in the Alentejo, is the garden of the old spa at Moura, built below the castle and with a wide variety of fountains, as well as a grand duckpond.

In the Algarve one of the best places to seek solitude is among the palms and fountains at Estói (see page 25), whose small park has some ancient shrubs as well as some of the best ornamental stonework in the country.

If you have children to amuse, try the gardens and the small zoo next to

The lush subtropical gardens of the 18th-century Palácio de Estói

the castle at Silves. They may also enjoy a visit to the lush gardens of the São Lourenço Cultural Centre, outside Almansil, while you try to explain what the marble sculptures represent.

Some of the region's most luxuriant natural vegetation can be explored around the spa town of Caldas de Monchique.

Prehistoric and Roman remains

If getting away from the 20th century altogether sounds appealing, the landscapes of the Alentejo and the Algarve can reveal much of southern Portugal's long history. In the Alentejo you can find some remarkable examples of prehistoric life deep in the countryside: try the tour on page 38 to discover the ancient stone circle at Almendres, the menhir of Zambujeiro and the underground cave paintings at Escoural, or look for more stone circles around Monsaraz.

Even in the Algarve, among the modern holiday villas, you can find evidence of Roman and even earlier life in the southwest corner of Iberia. Though neglected in the past, and sometimes difficult to find, the megalithic grave at Alcalar and the remains of the Roman villa at Abicada, near Portimão, are soon to be excavated further. You can find lots more to follow up in the fascinating regional museum in Lagos, which displays artefacts from neolithic, Bronze Age and Roman sites throughout the Algarve. Further east, the Roman remains at Milreu and at Vilamoura are better preserved and easier to interpret, while the ruins of Balsa can be found near the Torre de Ares, a medieval watch-tower on the

Memorial to the epic poet, Luís Camões

coast 5km west of Tavira. High in the mountains of the Serra do Malhão, the Pedras Alte dolmen stands near Mealha, also well known locally for its curious round buildings, now used as haylofts (N504 from Cachopo).

Roman tuna-fish mosaic, Milreu

Wildlife

Tourists were not the first temporary residents in southern Portugal: the Algarve in particular has long provided a rich variety of natural habitats which attract migrating birds. Despite the restrictions on hotel and resort development imposed by the Portuguese government's PROTAL programme, conservationists are concerned that many of those habitats are still under threat. An increasing awareness in Portugal itself, where environmental groups (such as the Liga Para Proteção da Natureza) are becoming increasingly active, has led to the designation and protection of several areas, some of which welcome visitors.

Largest and best known is the Parque Natural da Ria Formosa, an area covering 17,000 hectares, mostly of saltpans and lagoons stretching from Anção to Cacela Velha. This is an important stop-over and wintering point for migratory birds, as well as being rich in shellfish and a spawning ground for other fish. On a clear day you get a particularly good view of the reserve as you come in to land at Faro airport. Contact the park office at Rua Teofilo Braga 15–1, 8000 Faro (tel: 089 27514).

The sandy offshore islands east of Faro are particularly rich in bird life, so ornithologists, as well as beach-seekers, should take the ferry across, especially in spring.

In the very southeast corner of the Algarve, the Reserva Natural do Sapal de Castro Marim e Vila Real de Santo António lies between the Via Infante highway, the Guadiana river and the sea. It consists of saltmarsh *(sapal)* which can be explored along a series of

Cabo de São Vicente – renowned for its flora and bird life

The unusual saltmarsh broomrape

boardwalks. Like the Ria Formosa, it supports a wide range of bird life; for information, go to the office located in the 13th-century fortress in Castro Marim, up Rua do Castelo from the central Praça 1 de Maio.

Moving west, another excellent area for bird-watching, and an important collection of habitats, lies between Portimão and Lagos, at the heart of the developed coastline. The successful campaign to raise the Alvor estuary to the status of a natural reserve has been a long one and there are still threats from development: the local economy depends on fishing, and lunching on fresh fish near the *lota,* or fish market, at Alvor is popular with visitors; this is also a prime area for more hotel and golf-course development.

The best way to explore the Ria de Alvor is to visit the A Rocha field studies centre at Cruzinha, which lies a short way south of the N125, opposite the turning to Mexilhoeira Grande. The centre publishes a range of ornithological literature, such as *An Atlas of the Wintering Birds in the Western Algarve.*

A smaller area of natural interest, which is very popular with Lagoans and visitors alike, is the Sitio das Fontes, an inlet from the Arade estuary which lies about 2km from the turning to Estômbar village, between Lagoa and Portimão. Much more spectacular, Cabo de São Vicente (Cape St Vincent) has an abundance both of flora – particularly in spring – and bird life; seabirds and migrating land birds use it as a landmark and staging post. Further north, the underdeveloped coast of the western Algarve and the Alentejo are also ideal places for watching the wildlife undisturbed. A word of warning, however: when you are exploring more remote areas, whether in the Algarve or the Alentejo, remember to be alert to hunting – a very popular pastime, theoretically restricted to Thursdays and Sundays in season; stray gunshot is an all-too-real threat to life and limb.

The Algarve's attractive flora

Shopping

*T*he main challenge for the shopper in southern Portugal, particularly in the main tourist areas, is sorting out the quality goods from the tat. If you keep your eyes open you can pick up some real bargains, especially at local markets. Do not ignore roadside vendors: their home-made produce may be cheaper and better than the equivalent in shops. On the whole haggling is usually more trouble that it's worth, though it can pay off if you suggest a discount for buying more than one of any object.

Antiques

Antique objects, whether found in shops or in markets, tend to be expensive. Religious artefacts, old *azulejos* and Rato pottery predominate. The Casa da Papagaio (Rua de 25 Abril, Lagos) is a store worth visiting for its vast and eccentric array of odds and ends. It is presided over by two green parrots and has a less spectacular sister shop in Portimão (Rua Santa Isabel).

Baskets

Baskets are something of an Algarvian speciality but be sure to check that you are getting the real thing, since cheap Chinese imports now outnumber home-made products. Algarvian baskets are made from esparto grass, rushes or palm and come in many shapes and sizes. The main centres for their

Useful and beautiful Algarvian baskets

manufacture are Aljezur, Monchique and the village of Odeleite.

Cork and ceramics

Cork is one of the south's main exports, but its transformation into an assortment of tourist souvenirs is one of its most tacky and least satisfactory manifestations. Ceramics are a safer bet, with a fair variety of styles ranging from ubiquitous pottery roosters to antique *azulejos*. The local wares include simple terracotta kitchen vessels from the Algarve, decorative pieces from the Alentejo illustrated with naively painted scenes from everyday life and, from Estremoz, small figurines of saints and famous Portuguese characters.

There are many places from which to buy but there is a concentration of potteries along the N125 near Porches. The best examples of the delicate local floral-patterned wares can be found in the village of Porches at Olaria 7 (Rua da Junta 7; tel: 082 52858).

Food and wine

The many sweetmeats and pastries of the south are available everywhere and make excellent presents, especially when nicely wrapped, as do the local almonds and various dried fruits. Apart from the

Sturdy rush-bottomed furniture

strawberry-tree (arbutus) liqueur, *Medronho*, and the bitter almond liqueur, *Amêndoa Amarga*, there are several good southern wines, mostly red and mainly from the Alentejo. Vintners with large selections include two in Portimão: Tio José (Praça da República) and Casco Garrafeira (Rua João de Deus 24).

Handicrafts

Local handicrafts *(artesanato)* are well worth investigating both as souvenirs and for their practical value. The further you get away from the coast the better the quality is likely to be. In the Algarve the town of Loulé is very much the centre of traditional craft skills, specialising particularly in copper and brass pots, including the unique Algarvian cooking utensil, the *cataplana*. Up in the mountains the town of Monchique is also a good centre for handicrafts.

Leather

Leather articles are very good value,

especially when bought in open markets. Loulé is once again the place to go for fancy goods, such as decorated bridles and saddles. Clothes generally are much cheaper than in other parts of Europe. For those looking for quality, the Rua Santa Isabel in Portimão has a number of stylish shops, as does the Rua Santo António in Faro.

Textiles

The distinctive Arraiolos carpets can be purchased in the Alentejo from the town of the same name and also from outlets in Évora (Praça do Giraldo) and in Portimão (Rua Teofilo Braga). The town of Mértola has a small co-operative which produces hand-woven woollen rugs and blankets in marvellously vibrant geometric patterns using the natural colours of the wool. Their workshop can be found down some steps opposite the tourist office in Rua da República.

Less spectacular, but considerably cheaper, are the locally woven striped rugs found practically everywhere in the Algarve.

Crochet work was once a thriving cottage industry but it is now quite rare; asking around a village whether anyone still practices the craft can sometimes yield results. When it appears in craft shops it tends to be pricey.

Marketplace bargains

MAIN SHOPPING AREAS

ALBUFEIRA
Albufeira is the main package resort of the Algarve and its principal shopping street is the pedestrianised Rua 5 de Outubro, close to the seafront.

Casa e etc
A new store with a good selection of modern handicrafts and furniture.
Rua 5 de Outubro. Tel: 089 513690.

Charles Jourdan at St James
This exclusive shoe shop sells Paris-designed shoes but at considerably cheaper Portuguese prices.
Centro Turial. Tel: 089 515897.

Infante Dom Henrique House
A good place to go for ceramics both old and new.
Rua Candido do Reis 30. Tel: 089 593267.

ÉVORA
The Alentejo is almost completely uncommercialised compared with the Algarve but Évora has several good craft stores in or around the main square, the Praça do Giraldo.

Miranda Ferrão
Watches and jewellery, including local filigree work.
Rua 5 de Outubro 28–9. Tel: 066 22209.

Nazareth
Stationery on the ground floor, books (including several about the region) on the first floor.
Praça do Giraldo 46. Tel: 22221.

Stop
Another craft shop with a varied selection including 'naive' pottery from Redondo and lace from Évora.
Alarcova de Baixo 1. Tel: 066 23613.

Tapetes de Arraiolos
An *artesanato* (handicraft) store selling Arraiolos carpets, painted furniture and lace, plus a selection of Alentejan wines.
Praça do Giraldo 84–5. Tel: 066 20868.

Teresa Gormos
Outlet for fine crystal from Alcobaça, a town to the north of Lisbon.
Largo Luís de Camões 28 and 36.
Tel: 066 23695.

FARO
The capital of the Algarve has a good selection of shops centred around the pedestrianised Rua Santo António. There are also some interesting stores in the old part of town, near the cathedral.

António Manuel
A boutique with several branches in the same street, one of which sells high-quality leather jackets and boots.
Rua Santo António 51.
Tel: 089 822474.

Azularte
One of the best places to find good quality reproduction *azulejos*.
Rua D Teresa Ortigão 9.

Casa Branca
A large souvenir store selling ceramics, pewter and jewellery.
Rua Santo António 10. Tel: 089 26522.

Joaquim da Silva Carneiro
This large workshop near the cathedral sells antique ceramics and furniture as well as restored architectural salvage.
Rua da Porta Nova 6. Tel: 089 26156.

Oberon

A leather shop specialising in suitcases and handbags.
Rua Santo António 67. Tel: 089 823201.

LAGOS

The town has managed to retain its charm despite becoming a popular resort. Much of the centre of the town has been pedestrianised, with the Rua 25 de Abril the busiest of its shopping streets.

A Cave Garrafeira

An English-run vintners with a wide but discriminating collection of wines and spirits.
Rua 25 de Abril 49. Tel: 082 761158.

Helder Castanho

Handmade replica sailing boats, from recycled material.
Rua Conselheiro Joaquim Machado 37. Tel: 082 767580.

João Calado

Earthenware pottery, tiles and cork souvenirs.
EN124, Lagos. Tel: 082 52858.

Tridente

Swimwear and fishing equipment.
Rua Lima Leitão 25. Tel: 082 813475.

LOULÉ

This quiet town is a good centre for crafts if you are prepared to shop around. The main shopping streets are the Rua 9 de Abril, by the pseudo-Moorish covered market, the pedestrianised Rua 5 de Outubro and the Rua da Barbaça near the tourist office. The covered market itself is a good source of rustic earthenware plates and pots at very reasonable prices.

Caldeiraria Louletana

Metal workshop where you can see the objects being made.
Rua da Barbacã 28. Tel: 089 415516.

Casa Taxinha

Leather goods, belts, bags and fancy harnesses.
Rua da Barbacã 9. Tel: 089 415076.

Centro de Artesanato

Wide variety of handmade rugs, earthenware jugs, embroidered tablecloths and caravelles (sailing ships) carved from wood.
Rua da Barbacã. Tel: 089 415230.

José de Brito Barracha

A large outlet for copper and brass vessels, including liqueur-making stills and *cataplanas*.
Rua 9 de Abril 25 and 29. Tel: 089 416723.

PORTIMÃO

This major resort has a good selection of high-quality shops which are located between the Rua do Comércio and the Rua Santa Isabel.

Carla e Barone

A good selection of shoes and hand-bags.
Rua do Comércio 25–27. Tel: 082 25201.

Galeria Portimão

Modern art gallery which also sells Mary McMurtrie's series of books on the *Flowers of the Algarve*.
Rua Santa Isabel 5. Tel: 082 422965.

Porches Pottery

Hand-painted regional pottery and Algarve handicrafts.
EN125, Porches. Tel: 082 381668.

Markets

*S*hopping in covered food markets or at street stalls in the open air, is a great way to experience the hustle and bustle of Portuguese life at first hand. In the covered food markets traders are in direct competition with each other and call out encouragingly to the passing customers. If you want to eat really cheaply there is no better way than by purchasing the ingredients for a picnic as you wander through. Home-made produce, such as cheeses and honey, can usually be purchased more cheaply than in shops and is often fresher. The buildings themselves are often architecturally interesting, notably the mock-Moorish market at Loulé.

Outdoor markets vary from the lavish fairs that are set up especially for festivals and holidays to the regular markets that occur on a weekly or fortnightly basis. In both there is always a wide variety of goods on offer from food and clothes to pottery and cassette tapes. Vendors are eager to sell so this is where you will get the best bargains especially if you try haggling. Times can vary throughout the year so it is worth checking with the local tourist office. Look out also for fruit sellers who set up their stalls alongside roads and at which you can purchase cheap water melons, seasonal fruits and home-grown vegetables.

If you are staying at one of the coastal towns or villages it is worth while getting up as early as 7am to witness the fishing catch being brought in and auctioned off at the wholesale fish market. Albufeira is probably the easiest place to see this taking place, at the Fishermen's Beach in the old part of town. The sheer variety of fish, from the exotic to the fearsome, is astonishing.

Terracotta pots for the garden

Albufeira
Apart from the fish market, there is an outdoor market on the first and third Tuesday of each month by the Orada chapel.

Alte
Third Thursday of each month.

Alvor
Second Tuesday of each month.

Estói (near Faro)
Second Sunday of each month.

Évora
Second Tuesday of each month in the Rossio square near the Jardim Público (Public Gardens).

Fuzeta (near Olhão)
First Thursday of each month.

Lagos
A large outdoor market is held on the first Saturday of each month and special fairs are mounted in August, October and November.

Loulé
Every Saturday morning.

Moncarapacho (near Olhão)
First Sunday of each month.

Monchique
Second Friday of each month.

Olhão
Olhão has two big covered markets (one for fish and one for food) right next to each other on Avenida 5 de Outubro, fronting the Río (River) Formosa.

Paderne (near Albufeira)

Hand-crafted leather at bargain prices

First Saturday of each month.

Portimão
First Monday of each month, behind the railway station.

Quarteira
Large Gypsy Market every Wednesday.

São Bartolomeu de Messines
Last Monday of each month.

São Marcos da Serra
First Monday of each month.

Silves
Third Monday of each month.

Tavira
Third Monday of each month.

Vila Nova da Cacela (near Vila Real de Santo António).
Third Sunday of each month.

Entertainment

*T*here is no shortage of entertainment to be found in the Algarve, from visiting a cabaret to dancing the night away. On the whole, low-brow activities tend to outnumber high-brow ones but it does not all have to be mindless fun. During the summer months several music festivals are mounted which often feature artists of international renown. In recent years a number of art galleries have sprung up which display work by both contemporary Portuguese artists and by foreigners. Tourist offices are always the best source of information about local events, many of which are only publicised at short notice. The larger hotels also give out information and some even publish their own leaflets about forthcoming attractions. The fortnightly *Algarve News* is useful for listings, as is the monthly *Algarve Magazine*. In Portimão there is an occasional free information magazine, *Discover Portimão,* which has listings and restaurant reviews; it can be found at the tourist office and at art galleries.

ART GALLERIES

Apart from a few big names, contemporary Portuguese art is practically unknown outside of Portugal. In fact there is a thriving art scene and, in recent years, several interesting galleries have opened up dealing in a wide range of work, from the experimental to the traditional. Some of the best galleries for browsing and for buying are listed below.

Albufeira
Galeria Algarve, Pateo da Aldeia.

Beja
Escudeiro, Rua dos Escudeiros.

Évora
Cooperativa Gesto-Arte, Rua das Fontes.
Galeria Évora, Rua Manuel do Olival.

Faro
Galeria Nova Era, Avenue da República Federal Alema.

Galeria Trem, Rua do Trem.

Portimão
Galeria de Portimão, Rua Santa Isabel.
Galeria 44, Avenue São João.

Tavira
Casa das Artes, Rua João Corte-Real.

DISCOS AND NIGHT-CLUBS

Discothèques are to be found throughout southern Portugal. In the Algarvian resorts they vie with each other to attract custom with ever more sensational gimmicks. Things do not really start to happen until 1am but they can then continue until dawn. Entry prices at the height of the tourist season can be high.

Albufeira
Kiss
This is the biggest and the most frenetic disco in the area, usually staying open until 4am.
Areias de São João.

Locomia
A giant champagne bottle periodically
fills the dance floor with foam.
Santa Eulalia.
7½
Popular disco in the centre of town.
Rua Cais Herculano.

Évora
Lusitano
The liveliest part of the Lusitano Youth
Club.
Rua Serpa Pinto.
Slide
Slightly bigger disco in the same street.
Rua Serpa Pinto.

Faro
Barracuda
Disco on the beach.
Praia de Faro.
Olympus Disco
The most popular, if not the best.
Rua do Prior.

Lagos
Bon Vivant
Busy disco on three levels.
Rua 25 de Abril.
Lancarote Club
Combines restaurant, bar and disco.
Rua Lancarote de Freitas.

Le Privé
Currently the most fashionable place to
dance.
Praia de Luz.

CABARETS
The biggest and glitziest international
cabaret entertainment is to be found at
Michael's, which is in the Montechoro
leisure complex near Albufeira.
Modelled on Parisian-style shows, there
are dancing girls and singers as well as
magicians and clowns for the children.
You can book direct (tel: 089 55997) or
through your hotel.

CASINOS
For those with money to throw away the
Algarve has three casinos at Alvor,
Monte Gordo and Vilamoura which are
open from 5pm until 4am. The entrance
fee is about 1,500$00, passports or ID
cards must be carried and men are
required to wear jackets. Roulette,
blackjack and baccarat are played and
there are slot machines.
    There are also bars, restaurants and
live entertainment on the premises; these
can vary in quality but are consistently
expensive.

Foam parties are popular with disco-goers

Girls in festive dress

MUSIC AND CULTURE

The most moving and powerful music to be heard in the south is the three-part male voice singing of the Alentejo. Melancholy, slow and regular, the songs tell of the struggles of the land and the pain of death. A single voice intones the verse and is joined by the other voices in the chorus, the absence of any other accompaniment intensifying the rawness of the emotion. This type of singing is strongest in the Serpa district and around the village of Cuba.

Enthusiastic dancers in the traditional style

In the Algarve there is more enthusiasm for dancing than for singing. The best known of the region's dances is the *corridinho,* a kind of circular polka danced in pairs with much whirling of skirts and stamping of feet.

In Pechão, near Olhão, the traditional 'Dance of the Moors' used to be performed in September. This was similar to the *Mouriscas* (battle dances between Christians and Moors) found throughout the Iberian peninsula. These dances are now best seen at local fairs and festivals but they also get performed at organised folklore events and centres, such as the Fonte Pequena Folklore Centre, in the village of Alte, and at the Hotel Eva in Faro.

Fado has become so closely identified with Portugal, through the fame of its greatest exponent, Amália Rodrigues, that *fado* bars have appeared on the south coast. These gloomy ballads of love and death, accompanied by the plaintive Portuguese guitar, were originally from, and exclusive to, Lisbon. There are regular performances of *fado* at the Hotel Eva in Faro and at the Sol e Mar Hotel in Albufeira.

FADO BARS

Strictly speaking the melancholy songs of the *fado* are associated with Lisbon and Coimbra rather than the south of Portugal but, rather like flamenco in Spain, its tourist appeal is such that *fado* clubs have sprung up everywhere. Unfortunately performers can vary dramatically in standard. Venues include the Restaurant–Bar in Albufeira, the A Muralho restaurant and the Hotel de Lagos in Lagos.

FILMS

Most of the foreign films that come to Portugal are subtitled and not dubbed. Blockbuster films are shown in Portugal soon after they are released and there are several cinemas in the Algarve, but fewer in the Alentejo.

Beja
Cine-Teatro, *Largo de São João.*

Faro
Cinema Santo António, *25 Rua Santo António.*

Portimão
Cine-Esplanada (summer only) *Avenida 3, Praia da Rocha.*

FOLK MUSIC AND DANCING
Southern Portugal has a strong

Evening entertainments

indigenous music and dancing tradition and, in recent years, many traditional local customs have been revived for tourist consumption. This can mean that, like shopping for handicrafts, you will come across the good, the bad and the indifferent. Many resorts organise folk dancing displays in the summer evenings and September is the month of the National Folklore Festival. In Faro, at the Hotel Eva, there are weekly displays of folk dancing given by the Rancho Folclorico de Faro; ask at the reception for details. The village of Alte also has regular displays at the Fonte Pequena Folklore Centre. During the summer in Albufeira there is dancing almost every night in the Largo Eng Duarte Pacheco, starting at 10pm.

MUSIC

Apart from folk music and *fado* there are many other kinds of music to be found in the south. During May and June there is an Algarve Music Festival which is predominantly classical and involves both Portuguese and foreign artists. Events are held in venues right across the Algarve. Look out for listings in churches of organ recitals and choral concerts. Recorded rock music is impossible to avoid but major rock stars also perform live in the Algarve.

Fado singer gives an impromptu performance

NIGHTLIFE

Mass tourism has meant a steady proliferation of places for evening entertainment along the Algarve coast. The evenings are balmy and a gentle stroll along the seafront is pleasant enough, with bars and cafés open late during the summer. There is a wide selection of discothèques and clubs which range from the extremely raucous to the sophisticated. Discos, particularly, go in and out of fashion with amazing rapidity and many vie with each other in inventing increasingly outrageous gimmicks in order to attract custom. Those who wish to dance the night away will never be short of choice.

Few of the regular evening entertainments have an especially local feel – most aspire to a cosmopolitan flavour. The Algarve, as much as Lisbon, is on the international cabaret circuit and can attract top stars.

People with money to lose have the choice of three casinos, at Alvor, Vilamoura and Monte Gordo. A less risky pastime would be a trip to the cinema. English-language films are nearly always shown with their original dialogue plus Portuguese subtitles. Prices are inexpensive and there are cinemas at all the major resorts, often within the larger shopping centres.

The Alentejo does not cater for the tastes of international travellers in anything like the same way. Cinemas exist but are less plentiful than in the Algarve. In recent years the city of Évora has become a well-known centre for good-quality theatre, but performances are always in Portuguese.

Monte Gordo's casino

Albufeira by night

Invitation to dance in Vilamoura

Festivals

Scarcely a week goes by without some town or village in Portugal honouring a local saint or celebrating a local custom. Fairs, festivals and folk pilgrimages are all events worth catching, and the smaller the village the more jolly and intimate the occasion tends to be. Some of the dates of these festivities vary from year to year so it is worth checking with the tourist office before heading off into the back of beyond.

January
Between New Year's Day and Epiphany small groups perform New Year 'carols' in the streets.

February
The small Alentejan town of Mourão celebrates the Feast of the Purification of the Virgin with a festive procession on the second day of the month. The beginning of Lent, Shrove Tuesday, occurs at the end of February or the beginning of March. Carnival is the excuse for much lively activity through-out the country but the most splendid celebrations occur at the Algarve town of Loulé. The pagan origins of Carnival have to do with welcoming the spring and rejoicing at the death of winter. In Loulé this is marked by the 'Battle of the Flowers', when large flower-bedecked floats process through the town. This is also the time of year when the almond trees are in blossom. There is also an international cross-country race held at a different location in the Algarve each year.

March/April
The Mass of the Easter Vigil, celebrated late on the Saturday evening preceding Easter Sunday, often includes a grand procession with a band and floats, and sometimes flowers are strewn in the streets. In Loulé, at Easter, there is a unique *romaria* (pilgrimage) celebrating the Sovereign Mother (Mãe Soberana). An image of the Virgin is carried from Monte de Piedade to the church of São Francisco where it is kept for two weeks before being returned. On 25 April there is a national holiday to commemorate the 1974 Revolution which ended the dictatorship.

May
May Day is a national holiday; many towns and villages celebrate with folk festivals, of which the most picturesque is held in the Algarvian village of Alte. For the first three days of May the town of Estói has its own Festa da Pinha (Festival of the Pine), whereas the town of Vila Viçosa celebrates the last two days with a country fair. Salir celebrates the Festa da Espiga (Grain Festival) in the second week of the month.

May/June
The Algarve Music Festival: concerts, recitals and ballet performances across the province.

June
A national holiday, on 10 June, celebrates the poet Camões and Portuguese communities scattered throughout the world. On 13 June, the

Feast of Santo António, the Lisbon-born saint, is celebrated in many southern towns, especially in Reguengos in the Alentejo. The Feast of St John the Baptist (São João), another popular saint, is celebrated in various parts of the region on 23, 24 and 25 June; one of the biggest festivals is held in Évora over three days starting on 24 June.

July
Around 16 July the Feira da Nossa Senhora do Carmo, an important festival, is held in Faro to celebrate the Virgin's protection of fishermen. Silves is the setting for a beer festival held in the third week of the month and involves

Festival lights and festive crowds

music-making as well as drinking. From 18 to 26 July the tiny medieval town of Monsaraz stages a festival of music and handicrafts.

August
The small port of Olhão celebrates the plenitude of sardines and other fish by staging a Seafood Festival. In Castro Marim, on the Guadiana river, they celebrate the Feast of Our Lady of Martyrs between 15 and 17 August with a festival and a fair. In the Alentejo there are festivities at Castelo de Vide on 10 August and at Beha between 10 and 15 August.

September
This is the month of the Algarve Folk Music and Dance Festival, held across the province, which usually peaks at the middle of the month. In the Alentejo there are major fairs and festivities at Moura on 12 and 13 September, at Elvas from 20 to 25 September and at Viana do Alentejo from 26 to 28 September.

Dressed up to celebrate

October
A national holiday commemorating the founding of the Republic in 1910 occurs on 10 October. Faro stages another festival around 20 October in celebration of Santa Iria. In the mountain town of Monchique there is a big country fair between 26 and 28 October and an impressively large one is held in the small Alentejan town of Castro Verde on 18 October.

November
All Saint's Day on 1 November is a national holiday and All Soul's Day on 2 November is an important religious feast.

December
The first day of the month is the anniversary of the day in 1640 when the Portuguese restored one of their own to the throne after 60 years of Spanish rule. Christmas Day is celebrated as a religious feast in a restrained fashion.

Children

*T*here are considerably more activities for children in the Algarve than in the Alentejo. Many of these centre around the beach and related activities, such as pedaloes and windsurfing. Some of the bigger hotels organise a programme of activities for children which includes sports and games. Riding lessons are widely available (see Sports section). There are very few facilities, however, in terms of specific children's museums or theatres. Bored teenagers looking for action away from the beach are well served by such delights as snooker halls, mini-golf, bowling alleys and even video arcades in the larger resorts along the Algarve coast.

In the last few years improvements have been made and many new entertainment centres have opened primarily aimed at children, the most popular of which are the water parks that line the N125 across the Algarve. As well as massive water slides, which are the main attraction, these parks have bars and restaurants and can sometimes merit a whole day's outing.

WATER PARKS
The Big One
Swimming-pool with waves, water chutes and so on.
N125, Alcantarilha. Tel: 082 322827.

Slide and Splash
Pools, chutes and slides.
N125, Estômbar, between Portimão and Lagoa. Tel: 082 341685.

Atlantic Park
Pool with waves, chutes and thrilling slides.
N125, near Quarteira. Tel: 089 397282

There is also a water park on the main road (N260) between Beja and Serpa in the Alentejo.

MINI GOLF COURSES
Mini Golfe das Açoteias
A complete 18-hole course. 400$00 entry.
Turistico Aldeias de Açoteias, Albufeira.

Mini Golfe Dom Pedro
One of several sporting facilities.
Hotel Dom Pedro, Vilamoura. Tel: 089 313270.

Mini Golfe Hotel Algarve
Full course, 450$00 entry charge.
Praia da Rocha, Portimão. Tel: 082 235001.

For riding, watersports and all other sports see pages 154–161.

Food and accommodation
Restaurants are used to catering for children. Several have menus specially aimed at children, but even if they don't it is easy to find simple food that your child will eat. The Portuguese themselves tend to include their children in all social events. A child under eight years of age sharing a hotel room with its parents is entitled to a 50 per cent discount and many hotels will make arrangements for baby-sitting.

Sport

Southern Portugal is a paradise for sports enthusiasts. Rain is infrequent, the many beaches are ideal for watersports, there is a fine marina at Vilamoura and the Algarve boasts some of Europe's most outstanding golf-courses. The midday sun can be oppressive at the height of the summer, even with the Atlantic breezes, but many facilities stay open into the evening so it is possible to avoid the hottest times.

Manicured fairways

FISHING

It is possible to hire equipment for offshore fishing or for fishing in the large inland reservoirs. The big attraction of the Atlantic coast, however, is the potential for deep-sea or big-game fishing. This is expensive but increasingly popular and many new centres have emerged in recent years. Over 200 types of fish swim in these waters; the more spectacular include tuna, shark, bass, marlin, ray and conger eel. Previous experience is not necessary though anyone prone to seasickness should be cautious; the waters are calm in summer but can be rough in winter, the optimum time for fishing. Portimão and Vilamoura are the main centres and there are different rates for fishermen and spectators.

Algarve's Big Game Fishing Centre

This is one of the most professional outfits and is run by Rudolf Streur. Cruises begin at 9am and lunch must be ordered in advance.
Praça da República, Portimão. Tel: 082 25866. Marina de Vilamoura. Tel: 089 315666.

Big Game Fishing

A 13m long boat, the *Sant' Anna,* does a whole day's cruise. Lunch must be ordered in advance.
Marina da Vilamoura – Cais Q-12. Tel: 089 315666.

Mini Cruzeiros do Algarve

Established 15 years ago. Half- or whole-

day cruises in the 10m long boat, the *Top Norte*. Meals available.
Marina da Vilamoura. Tel: 089 302984.

GOLF

The attractions of golfing in the Algarve are numerous – the temperate climate, the beautiful surroundings and, above all, the quality of the courses, several of which are championship standard. Unfortunately some of the top clubs are so exclusive that getting a game is almost impossible and, if you manage it, extremely expensive.

The Portuguese themselves are passionate about football

Palmares

Designed by Frank Penninck, a par-71 course with fine views of the sea and of the distant mountains.
Lagos. Tel: 082 762953.

Parque de Floresta

A well-designed but difficult par-72 course set in hilly countryside.
Budens, 15km from Lagos. Tel: 082 65333/4/5.

Penina

This par-73 course, designed by Henry Cotton in 1966, has a beautiful setting and is used for major tournaments. Proof of handicap required.
Montes de Alvor, near Portimão. Tel: 082 415415.

Quinta do Lago

Designed by Bill Mitchell, this is an immaculately kept course which is heavily booked up and very expensive.
Almansil. Tel: 089 394782.

São Lourenço

An expensive and exclusive American-designed par-72 18-hole course. Owned by the Forte hotel group who

are building the São Lourenço Hotel there. To get a game it helps to be staying at the Penina Hotel or the Hotel Dona Filipa.
Quinta do Lago. Tel: 089 396522.

Vale do Lobo

Another Henry Cotton design, it has narrow fairways and a spectacular seventh hole on its Yellow Course which crosses two ravines.
Almansil. Tel: 089 393939.

Vilamoura Golf Club

Vilamoura I

Set among pine woods with views of the sea, this Penninck-designed course is one of the best in Europe.
Tel: 089 313652.

Vilamoura II

A combination of designers makes this a more unpredictable course.
Tel: 089 315562.

Vilamoura III & IV

Two American-designed courses with difficult water hazards. Lessons given. Restaurant.
Tel: 089 380722.

LAND SPORTS

Many Portuguese are keen sports fans and they support their international stars, such as Rosa Mota the world champion marathon runner, with great enthusiasm. Football is a national obsession, despite the poor performance of the national team in recent years. The top clubs are based in Lisbon and Oporto; there are no outstanding teams in the south, though there are professional league teams at Faro, Lagos, Portimão and Vila Real de Santo António. The atmosphere at a match is partisan but friendly; games are seen as family entertainment and the occasional bad behaviour is castigated by officials as 'English' – clearly a synonym for unruliness.

The Portuguese bullfight, or *tourada,* is less violent than the Spanish *corrida* and great emphasis is placed on the skilled horsemanship of the *cavaleiro.* Dressed in ornate 18th-century style costume, the *cavaleiro* has to place six *bandarillas,* or darts, into the bull's shoulders. To do this he must first goad the bull into attacking him before manoeuvring himself and his steed into a suitable position. The ease with which he does this and his proximity to the bull are both indications of his finesse.

When he is through, eight men enter the ring on foot. These are the *forcados,* whose acrobatic antics require foolhardy valour as well as skill. They line up in front of the bull and encourage it to charge them, at which point the leading *forcado* throws himself over the animal's head as the others pile on in an attempt to subdue it. Throughout the fight the animal's horns are padded and the bull is usually not killed publicly, but afterwards and out of sight.

For those who take an interest, the best fights take place in the Ribatejo region and in Lisbon but regular *touradas* are held in many parts of southern Portugal on Saturday evenings throughout the summer.

Dramatic encounters
between bull and
cavaleiro

PLEASURE CRUISES

For a leisurely time on the water, there are many pleasure cruises available.

Alegria

A motor launch that can take 90 passengers. Day-time cruises from Portimão or night-time discos around the harbour.
Tel: 082 461449.

Bom Dia

Traditional Portuguese two-masted sailing ship which sails along the coast from Lagos.
Tel: 082 764670.

Condor da Vilamoura

The *Condor da Vilamoura* is a tall ship which runs full- and half-day cruises along the Algarve coast.
Vilamoura Marina. Tel: 089 314070.

RIDING

There are many riding centres *(Centro Hípico)* across the region and most offer lessons to beginners.

Centro Hípico da Vilamoura

Stadium with jumps, cross-country riding and beach treks.
Estalagem de Cegonha, Vilamoura. Tel: 089 322675.

Quinta dos Amigos

Treks along the coast and tuition for beginners.
Almansil. Tel: 089 395269.

Windsurfing school in Monte Gordo

Tiffany's Riding Centre
Lessons for children and beginners.
Almadena, near Lagos. Tel: 082 96444.

Vale de Ferro Riding Centre
Scenic cross-country rides in the foothills of Monchique from well-equipped stables with 30 horses. Free pick-up service from Lagos and Portimão. Jeep Safaris on request.
Mexilhoeira Grande. Tel: 082 96444.

SAILING
The best facilities for boat hire are at the Vilamoura Marina. There are yacht clubs at Ferragudo (tel: 082 25810) and at Carvoeiro (tel: 082 57266).

SURFING AND WINDSURFING
The west coast has the best beaches for surfing, the south coast the best for windsurfing. There are many schools for windsurfing in the Algarve which will rent out boards as well as provide tuition.

Algarve Windsurfing Centre
Established 10 years ago. Provides equipment and expert instruction and is good for beginners of all ages. Also has equipment for waterskiing and sailing.
Praia Grande, Ferragudo. Tel: 082 461115.

Escola de Windsurf
Rents equipment and gives instruction; located in front of the Hotel Algarve.
Praia da Rocha, Portimão.

Escondidinho Windsurfing
Qualified instructors and good equipment.
Praia Grande, Ferragudo. Tel: 082 461037.

Fun for all the family

SWIMMING
The Atlantic Ocean has a powerful undertow and even experienced swimmers should exercise caution. Beaches with lifeguards operate a system of flags to indicate whether swimming is safe or not. Green indicates safety, yellow means take care and red is for danger. A blue checked flag shows that the lifeguard is no longer in attendance.

TENNIS
As well as the following tennis clubs, many of the bigger hotels also have courts.

Clube de Tenis
Ten all-weather courts.
Carvoeiro. Tel: 082 357847.

Rocha Brava Tennis Club
Ten all-weather courts plus two squash-courts.
Carvoeiro. Tel: 082 358856.

Vilamouratenis Center
Twelve courts, equipment hire, a pro-shop, a bar and a restaurant plus expert tuition combine to make this one of the top clubs in Europe.
Vilamoura. Tel: 089 302369.

WATERSPORTS

The combination of south-facing beaches, warm weather and cool waters makes the Algarve a perfect location for watersports. The calmer waters of the southern strip of coast make it ideal for swimming, snorkelling or for scuba diving. The main resorts have life-guards in attendance and a system of flags to indicate whether it is safe to swim. On the western coast, facing the Atlantic, the breakers can produce a strong undertow, so it is wise to be cautious.

Equipment for fishing from the shore, or from jetties, can be hired

The Algarve offers perfect conditions for watersports and facilities for everyone, from experts to beginners

in many resorts. Rather more exciting is to go deep-sea fishing in search of bass, marlin and tuna, or even for shark. No experience is necessary but a day's outing will be expensive. A more modest alternative is to try the local fishermen, who will sometimes take visitors out for a tour of the waters – whether for fishing or just for sightseeing.

There are many places from which to hire boats, both sailing dinghies and motor boats.

Windsurfing and waterskiing are also increasingly popular, while the western coast is something of a mecca for surfers, the beaches around the village of Carrapateira being especially fine.

An alternative to the sea for sporting enthusiasts is the number of large inland reservoirs that exist in the south, many of which have facilities for sailing and windsurfing. However, be warned that, in summer, there can be a dramatic drop in the water level as the reservoirs shrink.

Food and Drink

*E*ating out in Portugal can be a joy: the food is wholesome, it comes in large helpings and is usually inexpensive. There are many regional differences and specialities but fish dominates the menu, especially *bacalhau* (dried salted cod), the national dish; this, it is said, can be cooked in 365 different ways, one for each day of the year. Boiled potatoes accompany practically everything but cooked green vegetables are uncommon (except in soups), side salads being more usual.

There is a wide range of prices and it is easy to eat out well for very little money, although this is becoming increasingly difficult in the more touristy areas. Portions tend to be large and it is possible for two people to share a main dish *(uma dose)* or simply to have a half portion *(uma meia dosa)* per person.

In the listing of recommended restaurants the approximate cost of a two-course meal for one person with coffee and a glass of beer or wine is indicated by one of four symbols:

$	750$00–1,250$00
$$	1,250$00–2,000$00
$$$	2,000$00–3,000$00
$$$$	3,000$00–5,000$00

Bear in mind that shellfish *(mariscos)* is always a lot more expensive than an ordinary meal.

In the main resorts restaurants can stay open late but in the country it is not unusual for them to close by 9pm. The busiest time for dinner is 8pm. Lunch can begin as early as 12.30pm and it is unwise to order much later than 2pm.

RESTAURANTS IN THE ALGARVE

Several of these restaurants are located in the countryside, so it is advisable to telephone in advance to check opening times, to make a reservation and ask for more detailed instructions on how to get there.

ALBUFEIRA
$$$ A Ruina
A well-known building on Fishermen's Beach. Several floors, fresh seafood, unpretentious.
Cais Herculano. Tel: 089 512094.

$$$ Cabaz da Praia
Cliffside terrace with a fine sea view. Varied cuisine.
Praça Miguel Bombarda. Tel: 089 512137.

$$ O Penedo
Quality restaurant with terrace overlooking the beach.
Rua Latina Coelho 15. Tel: 089 587429.

A typically relaxed restaurant

ALMANSIL
$$$ O Tradicional
A 19th-century farmhouse specialising in French cuisine. Dinner only.
On the Almansil-Quarteira road. Tel: 089 399866.

$$ Restaurant Adega Cova
Good country cooking with kid a speciality.
Vale de Eguas. Tel 089 395281.

ALVOR
$$$ Colibri
Portuguese restaurant offering a variety of vegetarian dishes as well as steaks and *cataplana*.
Estrada de Alvor 14a. Tel: 082 458110.

CARVOEIRO
$$$ Fonte da Guerreíra
Excellent fish dishes – try the grilled fresh salmon.
Estrada do Farol. Tel 082 357051.

$$$ O Rústico
Traditional restaurant with charcoal grills and fish.
Caramujeira. Tel: 082 342933.

FARO
$$ A Doca
Central restaurant, specialising in grilled fish.
Avenida República 20. Tel: 089 25453.

$$ Bella Italia
Pizza and pasta dishes.
Rua Dr Fransisco Gomes. Tel: 089 826701

$$$$ Cidade Velha
High-quality local cuisine in the old part of the town near the cathedral.
Rua Domingo Guieiro. Tel: 089 27145.

English and local cuisine

$$$ Clube Naval
Harbour restaurant specialising in fish dishes.
Boca de Faro. Tel: 089 823869.

$$$ Dois Irmãos
Long-established restaurant serving excellent local cuisine.
Rua Terreiro do Bispo 20. Tel 089 823337.

LAGOA
$$$ Casa Velha
African-influenced specialities, such as Angolan prawns and chicken moamba alongside Portuguese staples in an old converted bakery. Be sure to book in advance.
Rua Mouzinho de Albuquerque. Tel: 082 342600.

$$ La Romance
Converted farmhouse specialising in local cuisine.
Quinta da Bomposta, on the old road from Portimão to Lagoa. Tel: 082 843177.

Portuguese Food

Delicious sheep's cheese pastries

Despite a wide variety of different regional dishes, the traveller in Portugal will find that a number of popular recipes feature on most menus. *Caldo verde*, for example, is a rich vegetable soup made from finely shredded kale that originated in the northern Minho region. *Bacalhau* (dried salted cod) is ubiquitous. The dishes you are most likely to find on the menu are *Bacalhau a Brás* (flaked with onions), *Bacalhau a Gomes de Sá* (flaked with potatoes and hard boiled eggs) and *Bacalhau com nata* (flaked with cream).

The outstanding Portuguese cheese, *Queijo da Serra,* is a sheep cheese from the Serra da Estrêla mountains. It has a smooth and subtle flavour like good brie. The choice of desserts on the menu will nearly always be restricted to *pudim flan* (crème caramel), *molotov* (a kind of fluffy meringue), *arroz doce* (rice pudding) and the self-explanatory *mousse de chocolate.*

Algarvian specialities
There is rather more to Algarvian cooking than grilled sardines and shellfish – delicious though these are. Many recipes are prepared using a *cataplana,* a round-bottomed pan with a similarly shaped lid attached by a hinge which preserves all the juices and flavour of *cataplana* dishes such as pork, *bacalhau* and clams. The Algarve has its own version of the refreshingly cold Spanish soup, *gazpacho,* which employs old bread, peppers, cucumber and tomatoes. *Caldeirada,* a fish soup or stew, is also very popular.

Perhaps the region's greatest claim to culinary fame is its sweets and pastries. Figs and almonds, a legacy of Moorish times, feature strongly here. One of the best-known confections is *Dom Rodrigo,* a very sweet mixture of egg yolk and ground almonds wrapped in twists of silver paper. Another is the *Morgado,* a sphere of glazed white sugar with a silver ball on top and a sweet almond paste inside.

Alentejan specialities
Being a poor region, nothing is wasted in the Alentejo. *Açordas* is made by soaking old bread to produce a delicious kind of soup that is flavoured with coriander and topped with poached eggs. Pork is one of the region's major exports and *Porco a Alentejana* is an appetising dish of marinated pork eaten with clam sauce. Small chicken pies are another speciality and there is a very good cheese that comes from the town of Serpa which is sweet and soft when eaten fresh but which also matures well.

Menu decoder
Many restaurants will provide a menu in

English, though translations are often a little eccentric. The following words and phrases should be useful.

faz favor	please!
queria...	I would like...
uma mesa	a table
para duas pessoas	for two people
ementa/lista	menu
pequeno almoço	breakfast
almoço	lunch
jantar	dinner
faca	knife
garfo	fork
colher	spoon
copo	glass
acepipes	starters
sopas	soups
entradas	first course
sobremesas	desserts
queijos e frutas	cheese and fruit
prato do dia	dish of the day
peixes	fish
mariscos	shellfish
caça	game
carne	meat
pão	bread
manteiga	butter
sal	salt
pimenta	pepper
salada verde/mista	green/mixed salad
para beber	to drink
cerveja	beer
vinho tinto/ branco	red/white wine
café	coffee
leite	milk
a conta	the bill
açúcar	sugar
alho	garlic
amêijoas	clams
arroz	rice
assado	roast
atum	tuna
azeitonas	olives
bacalhau	cod
bife	steak (not always beef)
borrego	lamb
cabrito	kid
camarão/ões	shrimp/s
caranguejo	crab
carapau	horse mackerel
cavala	mackerel
chouriço	smoked sausage
coelho	rabbit
costeletas	chops
couve	cabbage
estufado/a	braised
feijão verde	green bean
feijoada	bean stew
fiambre	ham
figo	fig
frango	chicken
frito	fried
gambas	prawns
gelado	ice-cream
laranja	orange
leitão	suckling pig
limão	lemon
linguado	sole
lulas	squid
maçã	apple
melão	melon
mexilhões	mussels
molho	sauce
morangos	strawberries
ostra	oyster
ovo	egg
pargo	bream
pescada	hake
pescadinha	whiting
pêssego	peach
presunto	smoked ham
robalo	bass
salmonete	red mullet
torrada	toast
uvas	grapes
vaca	beef
vitela	veal

LAGOS

$$ Cardápio
A friendly Portuguese-owned restaurant, specialising in charcoal-grilled fish dishes.
Rua 25 Abril 79. Tel: 082 761330.

$$$ Dom Sebastião
Elegant and cool interior with good varied cuisine.
Rua 25 Abril 20–2. Tel: 082 762795.

$$ Jota 13
Popular for its grilled seafood.
Rua 25 Abril 58. Tel: 082 762319.

$$$ O Galeão
Good international cuisine in a lively atmosphere.
Rua da Laranjeira 1. Tel: 082 763909.

$$ O Trovador
English-owned, pleasant atmosphere, international cuisine.
Largo Convento Senhora da Gloria. Tel: 082 763152.

LOULÉ

$$$ Avenida Velha
Long established Portugese restaurant, specialising in fresh fish.
Avenida José de Costa Mealha. Tel: 089 416474.

$$$$ La Réserve
Outstanding international cuisine with a French bias, located 20 minutes south of Loulé.
Santa Bárbara de Nexe. Tel: 089 99234.

$$ O Avenida
Friendly atmosphere, central but closed on Sunday.
Avenida José de Costa Mealha. Tel: 089 462106.

MONCHIQUE

$$ A Charrete
Friendly local restaurant with reasonably priced tourist menu.
Rua Dr Jamora Gil. Tel: 082 92142.

$$$ Bica-Boa
Luxuriant surroundings, good and varied cuisine.
Lisbon road. Tel: 082 92271.

$$$ Paraiso da Montanha
Regional cooking; chicken *piri-piri* is the speciality.
3km from Monchique on the Foia road. Tel: 082 92150.

PORCHES

$$$$ O Leão
Restored 17th-century farmhouse with walled garden; international cuisine.
Tel: 082 381384. Dinner only.

PORTIMÃO

$$$ A Lanterna
Specialising in seafood, especially smoked swordfish and fish soup.
Near the old Portimão bridge. Tel: 082 414429. Closed Sunday.

$$ Azie
Dutch-run Indonesian restaurant in the centre of town.
Largo 1 de Maio. Tel: 082 424223.

$$ Bonjour Goodnight
Near the old bridge, specialising in seafood; reduced prices at certain hours.
Rua Serpa Pinto 22. Tel: 082 422516.

$$$ Dona Barca
This restaurant specialises in fish dishes and Algarvian desserts.
Largo da Barco. Tel: 082 84189.

$$$ Iemanjá
Weird cave-like décor but serves
excellent seafood.
Rua Serpa Pinto 9. Tel: 082 423233.

$$ Mariners
Restaurant and pub in a fine 18th-
century building. Good value
international cuisine and special
children's menu.
Rua Santa Isabel 28. Tel: 082 25848.

$$$ O Bicho
Spacious restaurant specialising in
Portuguese cooking.
Largo Gil Eanes. Tel: 082 22977.

$$$ O Buque
Large interior, specialising in *cataplana*
dishes.
*Parchal, near the Ferragudo side of the
bridge. Tel: 082 424678.*

PRAIA DA ROCHA
$$ Taj Palace
Curry house offering the usual range of
Indian dishes and take-away service.
Avenida Tomás Cabreira. Tel: 082 418458.

QUARTEIRA
$$ Adega do Peixe
Spacious restaurant with a good view,
well-known for its fresh seafood.
*Avenida Infante de Sagres. Tel: 089
312686.*

SAGRES
$$ A Tasca
Local fishermen's café with excellent
food and good views.
Near the seafront. Tel: 082 64177.

$$ O Pescador
Quality seafood restaurant.
Rua Comandante Matosa. Tel: 082 64192.

SILVES
$$$ Moinho da Porto
Friendly restaurant serving local dishes
including chicken *piri-piri*.
Rua Moinho da Porto. Tel: 082 442204.

TAVIRA
$$ Beira Rio Bars and Restaurant
Restaurants, bars and snooker room in a
warehouse overlooking the river. Noted
for its garlic-flavoured quails.
*Rua Borda d'Agua da Asseca. Tel: 081
23165.*

$$ Bica
The friendly staff will cook dishes to
your taste.
*Rua Almirante Candido dos Reis 22–4.
Tel: 081 23843.*

$$$ Imperial
Well known for its chicken and rice
dishes.
*Rua José Pires Padinha 22. Tel: 081
322306.*

$$$ Ponto de Encontro
Portuguese restaurant with good
selection of regional dishes.
*Praça Dr António Padinha. Tel: 081
323730*

VILAMOURA
$$ Golden Ming
Excellent Chinese restaurant alongside
the yacht-filled marina. Booking advised
in summer.
Marina Plaza. Tel: 089 301082.

**VILA REAL DE SANTO
ANTÓNIO**
$$ Caves do Guadiana
Good for seafood Portuguese style.
*Avenida da República 89. Tel: 081
44498.*

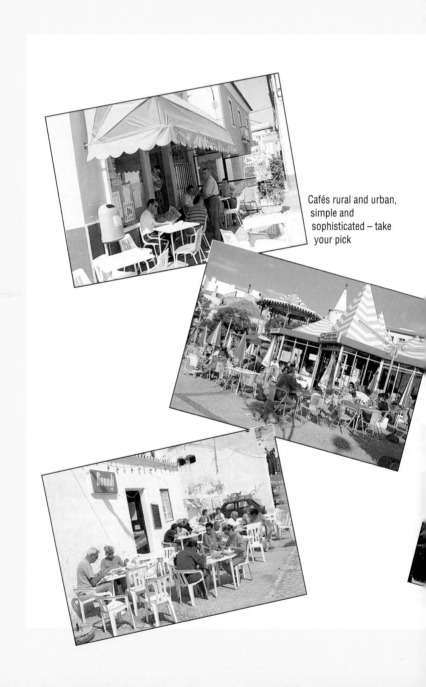

Cafés rural and urban, simple and sophisticated – take your pick

CAFÉ LIFE

The Portuguese café is a convivial place in which to spend some time; people drift in and out throughout the day as the mood takes them – sometimes for a quick snack, sometimes for a leisurely meal and other times just for a gossip. The atmosphere is warm and relaxed and it is perfectly acceptable to linger; you will not be hurried along, except occasionally at meal times if it gets particularly busy.

Those who are themselves in a hurry usually stand against the bar, which is very much the focus of café life. An air of bustle surrounds it, with the barman controlling the flow with an easy authority.

A confusing sight for the newcomer is the saucers of yellow seeds found along the tops of bars. These are *tremoços,* or lupin seeds, served free as an appetiser and eaten after being carefully squeezed from their skins. The unpractised often send them shooting around the room.

The Portuguese are a sweet-toothed nation which makes the *pastelaria* (bar/cake shop) another regular stopping-off point. It is not unusual for locals to start the day with the sweetest of sweetmeats plus a cup of coffee and even a glass of brandy! Despite the liberality of the licensing hours, drunkenness is the exception rather than the rule.

Along the south coast the tourist boom has seen the disappearance of many traditional eating places, such as the simple old *tascas,* or taverns, and their replacement with 'English' bars or even with fish and chip shops. Fortunately these are still in the minority and there remains a wide enough variety of Portuguese eating places to satisfy both residents and visitors alike.

Garlic – essential to Portuguese cuisine

RESTAURANTS IN THE ALENTEJO

BEJA

$$$ Restaurante Luís de Rocha
An old restaurant situated near the tourist office. One of its specialities is traditional Alentejan pork dishes.
Rua Capitão João Francisco de Sousa 63. Tel: 084 323179.

$ Salon de Thé Maltesinhas
This patisserie re-creates traditional Alentejo confectionery.
Rua dos Açoutados 35. Tel: 084 321500

ESTREMOZ

$$$ Aguias d'Ouro
Good restaurant in the town's main square, near the tourist office.
Rossio Marquês de Pombal 27. Tel: 068 333327.

$$$$ Pousada da Rainha Santa Isabel
One of the most attractive *pousadas* in Portugal with a wonderful location overlooking the town. Has a high reputation for comfort and excellent local cuisine. Reservations are essential.
Largo de Dom Dinis. Tel: 068 322075.

ÉVORA

$ A Muralha
Unpretentious café just off the main square.
Rua 5 de Outubro 21. Tel: 066 22284.

$$ O Antão
Good new restaurant serving local cuisine and exhibiting the work of local painters.
Rua João de Deus 5–7. Tel: 066 26459.

$$$$ Restaurante Fialho
Prize-winning restaurant located a little way from the centre but well worth seeking out.
Trav do Mascarenhas 16. Tel: 066 23079.

$$$ Restaurante Típico Guião
Tiled interior, good local cuisine.
Rua da República 81. Tel: 066 23071.

MÉRTOLA

$$$ Alsacrane
New restaurant serving local food, at the far end of town near the river.
Rua dos Combatentes da Grande Guerra 9. Tel: 086 62681.

ALMONDS

The pinky-white blossom of the almond trees in early February is one of the Algarve's most glorious sights, and an early sign that spring has arrived. The trees grow most abundantly in the Barrocal or limestone region of the Algarve although, as agriculture has diversified recently, they have sadly become less common.

An old local legend has it that a northern princess married to an Arab king became homesick for the snowy lands of her birth. In order to ease her grief her husband secretly planted almond trees as far as the eye could see. The following February, she saw the trees thick with blossom, thought the ground was covered with snow and was instantly cured of her heartache. In fact almonds probably existed in the province before the Muslim invasion. It is true, however, that the Arabs were the first to cultivate them and the Arab word, almond (*amêndoa* in Portuguese), has remained in use to this day.

The Portuguese make good use of the nuts which are harvested in August. In their simplest form they are eaten as appetisers, either roasted, fried or sprinkled with salt. They also appear on the Easter table in a thick coating of sugar along with the sugared white kernels of the *pinhão* nut – another Algarvian speciality – while the outer husks are traditionally burnt by potters in their kilns. Various harsh-tasting liqueurs are distilled from the almond, of which Amêndoa Amarga is probably the best known. Their greatest use, however, is in confectionary. There are few Algarvian sweets which do not include some form of almond paste. This is softer and sweeter than the marzipan of other countries, combining the almond with *ovos moles,* a gooey mixture of sugar syrup and egg yolks.

SERPA
$$ Cuiça e Filho
Cool and simple interior, good food.
Rua das Portas de Beja. Tel: 084 90566.

Juicy ripe melons

VILA VIÇOSA
$$ Os Cucos
Large modern restaurant in attractive wooded surroundings.
Mata Municipal. Tel: 068 98806.

Water from Caldas de Monchique

Portuguese Wines and Drinks

*A*part from Mateus Rosé and the lightly sparkling Vinho Verde, the wines of Portugal are not as well known as they should be. Several outstanding wines exist, such as the red Colares from near Lisbon or the red Barca Velha from the Douro valley in the north. The very best wines tend not to be exported so a trip to Portugal is a unique opportunity to drink well and inexpensively.

Serious regulation of the wine-producing industry began in 1756 when Portugal's chief minister, the Marquês de Pombal, established demarcated areas in order to improve standards. Today nine such areas exist, mostly in the north. In the south, the Setúbal area is demarcated, as is the southern strip of the Algarve.

Eminently drinkable Portuguese wines

The Alentejo has no demarcated region and, despite its size, only produces wines in a fairly compact area in the east of the province. The best of these are the full-bodied and fruity reds from Borba, Reguengos and Redondo. Alentejan white wines are not so highly regarded outside the province but are perfectly respectable, though they are probably at their best when still young. The vineyards of Beja, Vidigueira and Alvito all specialise in whites.

The Algarve does not produce any really top-class wines, though most of them are perfectly drinkable. Light, fruity reds predominate but the alcohol content is high, often more than 13°. Wines mainly come from the Lagoa, Portimão and Tavira areas. Lagoa also produces two sherry-like aperitif wines – Algar Seco and Afonso III. The well-known Algarvian liqueur, the powerful Medronho, is made from the strawberry-like berries of the *Arbutus unedo* tree. Other liqueurs use almonds (Amarguinha) and honey (Brandymel).

For a refreshingly light summer drink, Vinho Verde (green wine) is ideal. It is made in the northern Minho province and the 'green' of its name refers to its youth and not its colour, which can be white or red. It has a slight natural sparkle and a fairly low alcohol content.

Port, the drink most associated with Portugal, is also produced in the north – along the valley of the Douro river. It is a dessert wine which has been fortified with brandy. Most ports are a blend of wines from different years but a vintage port is a wine from an outstanding year which has been allowed to mature for as long as 20 years. Ruby port is young, full-bodied and sweet; tawny port, aged for longer, it less sweet and more

The vineyards of the Algarve

delicate in taste; white port is dry and best drunk chilled as an aperitif.

Non-alcholic drinks

Coffee drinking is a serious pastime for the Portuguese and there are several different ways of serving it. A small black coffee, like an espresso, is called *uma bica* and a small white coffee is *um garoto*. A larger cup of coffee made with milk is known as *uma meia de leite* and a tumbler full of frothed-up milk with a small coffee added is called *um galão*. If you want your *bica* diluted ask for *um bica cheia* and for a slightly milkier *galão* ask for *um galão de máquina*.

Portugal has many springs and spas and a wealth of bottled mineral waters. Your *agua mineral* can come *com gas* (sparkling) or *sem gas* (still) and its temperature can be either *frio* (cool) or *natural* (room temperature). Most of the spas are north of Lisbon but Caldas de Monchique in the Algarve produces a particularly healthy and refreshing water.

Hotels and Accommodation

Several types of accommodation are available in Portugal, ranging from the luxurious state-run *pousadas* to the smallest side-street *pensão*. If you have not booked in advance (necessary only in high season or in major resorts) it is worth checking out your options on arriving at your destination. A good *pensão* can often be better, as well as cheaper, than a hotel. In the unlikely event of finding all the official accommodation taken up, it is always worth enquiring about private rooms or flats for rent. Either ask at the tourist office or at a *pensão*.

Prices, no longer controlled by the state, vary enormously and will certainly be more expensive in the Algarve than the Alentejo. The tariff, listing the minimum and maximum charges according to the time of year, is attached to the back of each bedroom door. If you are travelling with a friend it is always cheaper to share a double room *(um duplo)* than for each of you to have a single room *(um quarto simples)*. A room with a double bed is called *um quarto de casal*. On signing in at a hotel you must submit your passport to the management for the purposes of official registration.

Pousadas

A *pousada,* which takes its name from the Portuguese verb *pousar,* meaning to rest, is the most exclusive and luxurious place in which to stay in Portugal.

Pousadas are owned by the state and run to the highest standards. The décor and cuisine reflect the customs and traditions

The de luxe Hotel Alvor Praia, Alvor

Some hotels have their own private beach for guests

of the area in which they are located. There are two types: regional *pousadas* are usually modern buildings situated in beautiful locations, such as the Pousada Santa Clara on the Alentejo/Algarve border; historic *pousadas* are converted buildings of historical significance, like the spectacular royal palace at Estremoz, now the Pousada de Reinha Santa Isabel.

Altogether there are 30 *pousadas* throughout Portugal, with eight in the Alentejo and two in the Algarve, but they are well distributed so that you can use them as bases for touring the regions. Only a few of them have more than 20 rooms so it is always wise to book well in advance. Booking is through the *pousada* organisation ENATUR, Avenida Santa Joana Princesa 10, 1700 Lisboa. Tel: 01 233 0933. Fax: 01 805846.

Hotels

Portugal has five different grades of hotel, ranging from the deluxe five-star category down to one-star. The grading is an official judgement of their quality

and facilities. A five-star hotel will have a wide variety of services, ranging from top-quality food and sports facilities through to in-house entertainment and, in some cases, even private beaches. As the stars decrease, so do the amenities but most hotel rooms down to two-star have an *en suite* bathroom with bath. In all hotel categories, down to one-star, you will usually find that the accommodation is clean and the service efficient. Many hotels have a complaints book, but any serious inadequacies should be reported to the nearest tourist office. Service charges and taxes are nearly always included in the bill but it is customary to leave a small tip.

In the Algarve, self-catering hotels are especially popular. These often form part of a large complex, with all the facilities of a conventional hotel, but the guests are housed in a self-contained apartment or in a villa. They can be very cost-effective and are particularly good for families.

Pensions

In Portugal a pension is called a *pensão* (plural: *pensões*). They are found in most towns and villages and they provide more modest accommodation than a hotel, though they too are graded and awarded up to three stars. It is always wise to inspect rooms and washing facilities before deciding to stay. Standards are usually good, however, and many *pensões* are as well equipped as a small hotel, while being considerably cheaper and often with a cosier and more friendly atmosphere. Some have restaurants but most only serve a fairly meagre breakfast of bread and coffee. A *residência* is similar in price and quality

The Hotel Penina Golf in Alvor

to a *pensão* but an *albergaria* or *estalagem* is in the middle price bracket.

Country houses and manor houses

Visitors seeking the seclusion of the countryside, combined with the comfort of a fine, often traditional, Portuguese house, should investigate Turismo de Habitação. This scheme, supervised by the Portuguese tourist ministry, provides grants for owners of historically significant or beautifully located houses to create facilities for visitors.

There are three categories of property: Turismo de Habitação itself offers manor houses or architecturally distinguished buildings in which to stay; Turismo Rural provides properties usually in or near to country towns; while Agroturismo uses farmhouses or farm buildings and offers visitors the chance to be involved in the work of the farm. In general the scheme provides an ideal way of getting to meet Portuguese people. Breakfast is provided and other meals can be requested. Booking is necessary and payment must be made in advance. The scheme originated in the Minho region but there are many fine places to stay in the south, though they can vary enormously in quality. You should book directly with the owners or through the following associations:

ACT – Associação das Casas em Turismo, Alto da Pampilheira, Torre D–2,3 A–2750 Cascais. Tel: 01 284 2901 or 01 284 4464.

PRIVETUR – Associação Portuguesa de Turismo de Habitação, Rua Castilho 209-1. Ft-1000 Lisboa. Tel: 01 654953.

Accommodation in the Loíos monastery

Top hotels all have pools

Reservations: Pan Europa. Tel: 01 563401. Fax: 01 522912. Telex: 16728.

TURIHAB – Associação do Turismo de Habitação, Praça da República, 4990 Ponte de Lima. Tel: 058 942729. Fax: 058 941864. Telex: 32618.

Youth hostels
There are less than 20 youth hostels *(Pousadas de Juventude)* in Portugal but the south boasts two of the best – at Sagres and at Évora. In order to stay you must have a valid International Youth Hostel Association card. Officially you can only stay for three nights but this can be extended if space permits. The charge is nominal and for a small extra fee you can hire sheets and blankets. For further information contact the Associação de Pousadas de Juventude, Av Duque de Ávila 137, 1000 Lisboa (tel: 01 355 9081).

Camping
There are over 100 campsites in Portugal, many of them in outstanding locations and all at a very reasonable rate (for further details see **Camping** on page 179).

Practical Guide

ARRIVING
Passports
Visitors from EU countries, North
America, Australia and New Zealand
only need a passport to enter Portugal.
A visa is necessary if you intend to stay
in the country for more than two months
(three months for Australians).

By air
Southern Portugal has two major
airports. The one at Lisbon (15 minutes
from the city centre) would be the
appropriate starting-off point for visiting
the Alto (Upper) Alentejo, whereas Faro
airport (about 15 minutes from town)
would be suitable for visitors to the
Algarve and the Baixo (Lower) Alentejo.

Faro is the larger airport but both are
well equipped with post offices, shops,
bars, restaurants and car rental facilities.
Both are linked to their respective cities
by regular bus and taxi services.

By boat
Brittany Ferries in England operates car
ferry services between the British port of
Plymouth and Santander in northern
Spain. The sea journey takes
approximately 24 hours and operates
twice a week during the summer. The
drive from Santander to southern
Portugal is just over 1,000km.

By train
There is a train service available daily
from London (Victoria) for Lisbon
(Santa Apolonia) via Paris and Irun in
northern Spain. The journey takes
about 38 hours and involves changing
trains (and stations) in Paris. A Motorail
service runs between Paris (Gare
Austerlitz) and Lisbon during the
summer. Passengers and cars travel
on different trains with the car train
arriving in Lisbon a day later.

By road
Driving to southern Portugal can involve
a long and exhausting journey (it is over
2,000km from one of the French
Channel ports to Lisbon, for example)
and you may find it cheaper to fly to
Portugal and hire a car on arrival. Twice-
weekly coach services to Lisbon and to
the Algarve are run by Eurolines in the
UK (tel: 0990 808080) departing from
London's Victoria coach station. Both
journeys take just under two days.

Boarding at Faro airport

CAMPING

Camping is a good option in Portugal since it is cheap and the 100 or so campsites are well kept and well situated. Sites are graded by the Ministry of Tourism and there is a camping booklet, *Roteiro Campista,* available from tourist offices and bookshops. Some of the camps are large enough to accommodate up to 5,000 people and have furnished chalets available for rent as well as shops and sports facilities. Passports must be left for the duration of your visit.

Camping away from official sites is not really approved of and is forbidden on beaches, in urban areas and within 1km of a camping site. For further details contact Federação Portuguesa de Campismo, Rua da Vaz do Operário I, 1010 Lisbon (tel: 01 8126890).

CHILDREN

The Portuguese are demonstratively affectionate with their own children and quite enthusiastic about other people's. Facilities for the amusement of children are much more plentiful in the Algarve than in the Alentejo. Several hotels provide specific entertainment for children and some offer baby-sitting.

Supermarkets sell all the necessities, including disposable nappies, for baby care, but remember that these will be harder to find in the depths of the country. The only real danger to children's health is intense sunlight, so avoid prolonged exposure to the sun.

CLIMATE

Portugal is a temperate country but very sunny, especially in the south. June, July and August are the hottest months of the year with the temperature rising as high as 30°C. Along the coast expect cool breezes in the evenings.

Spring starts as early as February. April and May are the best months to witness the splendid array of wild flowers. Summer is prolonged and it is still warm in late September. In recent years. October has been marked by heavy rainfall in the south, and in 1989 flooding washed away the old bridge at Tavira in the Algarve.

Weather Chart Conversion

25.4mm = 1 inch

$°F = 1.8 \times °C + 32$

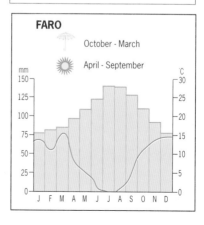

FARO

October - March

April - September

Conversion Table

FROM	TO	MULTIPLY BY
Inches	Centimetres	2.54
Feet	Metres	0.3048
Yards	Metres	0.9144
Miles	Kilometres	1.6090
Acres	Hectares	0.4047
Gallons	Litres	4.5460
Ounces	Grams	28.35
Pounds	Grams	453.6
Pounds	Kilograms	0.4536
Tons	Tonnes	1.0160

To convert back, for example from Centimetres to inches, divide by the number in the third column.

Men's Suits

UK	36	38	40	42	44	46	48
Rest of Europe	46	48	50	52	54	56	58
US	36	38	40	42	44	46	48

Dress Sizes

UK	8	10	12	14	16	18
France	36	38	40	42	44	46
Italy	38	40	42	44	46	48
Rest of Europe	34	36	38	40	42	44
US	6	8	10	12	14	16

Men's Shirts

UK	14	14.5	15	15.5	16	16.5	17
Rest of Europe	36	37	38 39/40	41		42	43
US	14	14.5	15	15.5	16	16.5	17

Men's Shoes

UK	7	7.5	8.5		9.5	10.5	11
Rest of Europe	41	42	43		44	45	46
US	8	8.5	9.5	10.5	11.5	12	

Women's Shoes

UK	4.5	5	5.5	6	6.5	7
Rest of Europe	38	38	39	39	40	41
US	6	6.5	7	7.5	8	8.5

CRIME

Petty crime has increased greatly in recent years but it is still not a serious problem compared with many tourist resorts. Be on your guard against pickpockets in crowded places; and never leave anything of value in your car, wherever you park it. Car radios are particularly at risk. Never leave valuable possessions unattended on a beach. In hotels it is usually possible to leave valuables in the hotel safe. Crimes should be reported to the Policia de Segurança Pública. In tourist areas some wear red armbands with CD on them. For police assistance tel: 115 or 112.

CUSTOMS REGULATIONS

Visitors to Portugal may bring in clothing and other objects, such as a camera or a bicycle, as long as it is for personal use only. The same applies to small quantities of food with the exception of meat. Up to 2 litres of wine (EU), 5 litre (non-EU); 1½ litres of spirits (EU), 1 litre (non-EU); and 200 cigarettes (non-EU), 300 (EU) are also allowed. There is no limit to the amount of currency that can be brought into the country, but sums exceeding the equivalent of 100,000$00 in foreign currency must be declared on arrival. When leaving you may take out foreign currency up to the amount imported and declared. Domestic animals may only be brought into the country if accompanied by medical documentation to show that they are free from all serious diseases (rabies, distemper etc). However, their return may be subject to quarantine.

DISABLED TRAVELLERS

Both Air Portugal (TAP) and British

The Guadiana river ferry linking the
Algarve with Spain

Airways have facilities for the disabled
such as wheelchairs at airports and
transfer chairs. If you are taking a
charter flight you should check with your
travel agent whether comparable
facilities are available. The Portuguese
Railway (CP) has carriages with toilets
adapted for wheelchair use and it gives
priority to wheelchair users in the
reservation of carriages. Large towns
have some marked parking places for
disabled drivers and these can be used
by foreigners if their car is suitably
marked. Tourist buses (Carris and Frota
Azul Barraqueiro) can be hired which
have facilities for the disabled.

Wheelchair hire can be found in most
towns at Centros de Enfermagem
(Nursing Centres). Consult your nearest
tourist office or the reception of your
hotel for the nearest one.

For further information and advice in
the UK contact the Royal Association
for Disability and Rehabilitation
(RADAR), 12 City Forum, 250 City
Road, London EC1V 8AB, tel: (0171)
250 3222.

The following is a selection of hotels
with easy wheelchair access.
Albufeira Hotel Montechoro,
Hotel da Aldeia.
Évora Estalagem dos Templarios.
Faro Hotel de Faro.
Lagos Hotel Golfinho, Hotel Meia
Praia.
Monte Gordo Hotel Alcazar.

DRIVING
To drive your own car in Portugal
you must carry a valid driving licence
and the vehicle registration documents.
An international insurance certificate
(or green card), though not compulsory,

is strongly advised. You should also carry a red warning triangle, which must be displayed 30m back from the rear of your car in the event of a breakdown or accident.

The Portuguese drive on the right-hand side of the road and use the international road sign system. Seat belts are compulsory and it is customary to sound your horn when overtaking.

Despite much new road building, road surfaces and conditions generally are very variable. Bear in mind that in the country people still travel by donkey (or on foot) and it is common to find flocks of sheep or other livestock crossing a road. Portugal's drivers are statistically the worst in Europe but most accidents occur on the main Lisbon/Oporto road and on the Lisbon/Algarve road. Behaviour tends to

Beware – unexpected road hazards!

be particularly reckless on motorways, but overtaking on corners is also common, as is the tendency to ignore pedestrians on crossings.

Petrol is expensive and unleaded petrol is still not easy to find away from main roads. Petrol stations are numerous especially on the N125, the Algarve's main east/west highway, but do not assume that they will all take credit cards. The N125 also has a number of orange SOS telephones in case of breakdown.

For more information contact the ACP (Automóvel Clube de Portugal) which has a reciprocal arrangement with other motoring associations, such as the British AA and RAC. It has a branch office in Faro and breakdown garages in Lagos and Portimão which are open daily 8am–12.30pm and 2–6pm.

ELECTRICITY
The current throughout southern Portugal is 220 volts AC and sockets accommodate the circular two-pin continental-style plug.

EMBASSIES AND CONSULATES
Australia Avenida da Liberdade 244–2 e4, 1200 Lisbon (tel: 01 523066).
Canada Avenida da Liberdade, 144–56, 1200 Lisbon (tel: 01 347 4892); Portimao (tel: 089 803757).
Ireland (consulate) 1 Rua da Impresa, 4th Floor, Lisbon (tel: 01 661569).
UK (embassy) 35–7 Rua São Domingos à Lapa, 1200 Lisbon (tel: 01 3924000); (consulates) Largo Francisco A Mouricis, Portimão (tel: 082 417800).
USA (embassy) Avenida Forças Armadas, 1600 Lisbon (tel: 01 727 3000300).

EMERGENCY TELEPHONE NUMBERS
All emergency services: 115.
Hospitals: Lagos (tel: 082 763034/6);
Portimão (tel: 082 415115);
English-speaking dentist: Almansil
(tel: 089 95453).
**Thomas Cook travellers' cheques
loss or theft:** 0505 449095 (freephone).
Emergency local assistance can also be
obtained from branches of Star Vigens
S.A. (Thomas Cook network member)
in Lisbon and Porto. A full list of
addresses can be found on page 190.

HEALTH
No vaccinations are needed for a visit to
Portugal. There is no free tourist medical
service but EU citizens can obtain a
refund of the costs using a form E111
(available from post offices and Health
and Social Security offices in your own
country before your visit). Medical
insurance is still advisable. Remember to
keep all your receipts for making a claim.

The most common medical
complaints are stomach upsets caused by
a sudden change of diet (though
Portuguese food is not particularly oily)
and over-exposure to the sun. Break
yourself in gradually to sunbathing and
always use suntan oils or lotions.

Ask at your hotel or at a tourist office
if you need a doctor or a dentist. At the
chemist *(farmácia)* there are fully
qualified staff who can deal with all
minor ailments. If the chemist is closed
there will be a list on the door telling
you where to find the nearest one that
is open.

HITCH-HIKING
Hitch-hiking is legal but quite difficult
from major towns. Country people are
often friendly and responsive but seldom
travel very far. Women travelling alone
should avoid hitching on motorways
alone at night.

LANGUAGE
Portuguese is a Romance language
(derived from Latin), so that you will
find some written words familiar if you
already have a knowledge of Italian,
Spanish or French. On the other hand,
the nasal pronunciation and the rapidity
with which it is spoken can make
comprehension quite difficult. Many
Portuguese speak English but your
attempts to master a few phrases
will be appreciated.

Pronunciation
Words ending in the letter **m** sound like
a combination of **n** and **m** so that **sim**
(yes) should be pronounced **seeng** (but
without really sounding the **g**). When the
tilde accent (˜) appears over the letters
ao, as in **não** (no), it sounds like a nasal
ow with a hint of an **oo** sound following.
The same accent over **ae**, as in **mãe**
(mother), sounds like the **y** of **my**.

The consonants **lh** when combined,
as in **talha** (butcher), sound like the **ll** in
million. The combination of **nh**, as in
banho (bath), sound **ny** like canyon.
The **j** of **queijo** (cheese) sounds like the
s of pleasure. The letter **s** before a
consonant, or at the end of word, should
sound like the **s** of **s**ugar; thus **Lisboa**
(Lisbon) is pronounced **Leeshboa**.

As in French, nouns have either a
masculine or a feminine ending and must
agree with the preceding article;
for example;

uma rapariga	a girl
a rapariga	the girl
um carro	a car
o carro	the car

The plural is usually made by adding **s** to the noun and to the definite article eg as;

as raparigas	the girls
os carros	the cars

Numbers

1	**uma(f), um(m)**	19	**dezenove**	
2	**duas(f); dois(m)**	20	**vinte**	
3	**três**	21	**vinte e um**	
4	**quatro**	30	**trinta**	
5	**cinco**	40	**quarenta**	
6	**seis**	50	**cinqüenta**	
7	**sete**	60	**sessenta**	
8	**oito**	70	**setenta**	
9	**nove**	80	**oitenta**	
10	**dez**	90	**noventa**	
11	**onze**	100	**cem**	
12	**doze**	101	**cento e um**	
13	**treze**	200	**duzentos**	
14	**catorze**	500	**quinhentos**	
15	**quinze**	1000	**mil**	
16	**dezesseis**	2000	**dois mil**	
17	**dezessete**	1,000,000	**um milhão**	
18	**dezoito**			

Days of the week

Sunday	**domingo**
Monday	**segunda-feira**
Tuesday	**terça-feira**
Wednesday	**quatro-feira**
Thursday	**quinta-feira**
Friday	**sexta-feira**
Saturday	**sabado**

Useful words and phrases

yes/no	**sim/não**
hello	**olá**
good morning	**bom dia**
good afternoon/night	**boa tarde/noite**
goodbye	**adeus**
please	**por favor**
thank you	**obrigada (f)**
	obrigado (m)
you're welcome	**de nada**
today	**hoje**
tomorrow	**amanhã**
yesterday	**ontem**
I am English	**sou Inglês**
do you speak English?	**fala inglês?**
how are you?	**como está?**
what is your name?	**como se chama?**
my name is...	**chamo-me...**
very well/good	**muito bem/bom**
see you later	**até logo**
where is...?	**onde é...?**
what/when	**que/quando**
why/how	**porquê/como**
how much is...?	**quanto é...?**
is there?/there is...	**há?/há...**
near/far	**perto/longe**
here/there	**aqui/ali**
is there a pension near here?	**há uma pensão aqui perto?**
old/new	**velho/novo**
cheap/expensive	**barato/caro**
open/closed	**aberto/fechado**
right/left	**direita/esquerda**
for/to	**para**
sorry	**desculpe**
excuse me	**com licença**
I don't understand	**não compreendo**
I would like...	**queria...**
large/small	**grande/pequeno**
more/less	**mais/menos**
do you have...?	**tem...?**
vacant rooms	**quartos vagos**
for two persons	**para duas pessoas**
for one night/week	**para uma noite/semana**
do you know...?	**sabe...?**
could you...?	**pode...?**
the key	**o chave**
bathroom/toilet	**casa de banho**
the bill	**a conta**
ticket/s	**bilhete/s**
stamp/s	**selo/s**

railway station	**estação de combois**
bus station	**estação de camionetas**
church	**igreja**
what do you call this in Portuguese?	**como se diz isto em Portugues?**
please write it down	**escreva-mo, por favor**
what time is it?	**que horas são?**

LAUNDRY

If you are staying in a hotel it is likely to provide a laundry service. There are very few self-service launderettes in Portugal but there are many laundries _(lavanderias)_, while some grocery stores, and even small post offices, sometimes offer a service. Your clothes will come back immaculately cleaned and ironed but be warned: Portuguese soap powders are often strong and may reduce the life of your clothes.

LOST PROPERTY

Most towns have a lost property office whose whereabouts can be obtained from tourist information centres.

MAPS

Many new roads have been built in southern Portugal in recent years so that maps can become out of date very rapidly. The Automóvel Clube de Portugal produces a good comprehensive road map and the Michelin map for Portugal (Number 437) is regularly revised. Town plans and local maps are usually available free from tourist offices.

MEDIA

There are several newspapers and magazines written for the English-speaking visitor to Portugal. The _Anglo-_

Portuguese News is really aimed at the expatriate community but the fortnightly _Algarve News_ has much useful and topical information. There is also the glossy bi-monthly _Algarve_ which is interesting. Tourist offices, and even hotels, sometimes produce newsheets about forthcoming local events.

All the major international papers are available in the larger towns a day after their publication but the _International Herald Tribune_ and _The Guardian_ can arrive on the day they are printed.

MONEY MATTERS

The _escudo_ is the Portuguese unit of currency; it is divided into 100 _centavos_. The monetary symbol is the dollar sign, which is written between the _escudo_ amount and the _centavos;_ thus 10$50 is

Exchanging news the old-fashioned way

10 *escudos* and 50 *centavos*. One
thousand *escudos* is known as a *conto*.

There is no limit to the amount of
money you can bring into the country.

Banks are open Monday to Friday
from 8.30am to 11.45am and 1pm to
2.45pm. A commission is charged for
changing money and it is advisable to
take your passport with you. Many of the
larger hotels will also change money.

NATIONAL HOLIDAYS

1 January	New Year's Day
Variable	Shrove Tuesday
25 April	Liberation Day
1 May	Labour Day
Variable	Feast of Corpus Christi
10 June	Portugal Day
15 August	Assumption of the Virgin
5 October	Republic Day
1 November	All Saints' Day
1 December	Restoration (of Independence) Day
8 December	Immaculate Conception
25 December	Christmas Day

OPENING HOURS

Shops are open weekdays 9am or
10am–1pm and 3–6pm. Saturday
morning is the busiest and most popular
time for shopping. Apart from major
shopping centres, shops are closed on
Saturday afternoon and Sunday. Most
museums and galleries are open Tuesday
to Sunday, 10am–5pm but closed on
Mondays. Some museums close for
lunch. If you find a church or castle
closed then go to the nearest bar or shop
where you can usually track down the
person responsible for the key.

PHARMACIES

See Health, page 183.

PLACES OF WORSHIP

St Vincent's Anglican Church organises
Sunday services at a number of places in
the Algarve. For details telephone the
following:
Albufeira (089) 589591
Lagos (082) 789126
Portimão (082) 414182
São Brás (089) 397938
Chaplain (089) 366720

Roman Catholic services are held at
St Andrews Penina; details from the
Penina Hotel, tel: (082) 239636. Mass
in English is celebrated at Santa Maria
church, Lagos and at Vilamoura Church.

The International Christian
Fellowship meets each Sunday at 11am
in the Evangelical Baptist Church,
Avenida 25 de Abril, Portimão and at
10am at Rua José Paleti 7, Lagos (tel:
(082) 495243).

The International Evangelical
Church (interdenominational) meets
every Sunday at 10.30am at Vale do
Judeu, just north of the EN125 between
Vilamoura and Quarteira (turn at sign by
'Longa Vida'), tel: (089) 328635. Also
children's Sunday School and crèche.

Dutch Protestant services are held in
several locations. Further details from
Dr Wooldrik, tel: (089) 514518.

A typical Alentejan church

Azulejo street sign in Albufeira

POLICE

The police are quite numerous in towns and are generally helpful. They wear dark blue uniforms (brown in the country) and are responsible for public order and for traffic control. A red arm band indicates an ability to speak another language.

POSTAL SERVICES

You will find at least one post office *(correio)* in each town and a few exist in villages. They are open weekdays 9am–6pm and Saturday 9am–1pm, but smaller branches tend to close for lunch and on Saturday. Stamps *(selos)* can also be bought in shops displaying a *correios* sign. Portuguese stamps are not gummed, so glue and brushes are provided! *Poste restante* mail can be sent to any post office in the country. It must bear the recipient's name, the address of the post office and be marked Lista da Correios.

PUBLIC TRANSPORT

Air

The internal airlines TAP, Air Portugal and Portugália connect Lisbon, Porto, and Faro. Portugália operates an airbridge commuter service between Lisbon and Porto or Faro. No advance booking is necessary, you just need to turn up.

Bus

Bus travel is the cheapest way of getting around Portugal. The nationalised bus company, Rodoviária Nacional, can take you to almost every town in the country. For regular bus travel within one city it is possible to obtain tourist passes which are valid for all forms of public transport.

Bus stops are marked *paragem;* buses will not stop unless you extend your arm.

Trains

Although the state-run railway system, Caminhos de Ferro Portugueses (CP), has not been modernised for many years, it is comprehensive and cheap – if a little slow.

Children under four travel free if they do not occupy a seat. Children under 12 pay half price. Senior citizens (over 60) receive a 30 per cent reduction on the production of a passport or other valid ID providing proof of age. There are also weekly and fortnightly passes valid for all trains. Car carriage by train has to be arranged at least 15 days in advance.

The Sotavento train from Lisbon to Faro runs every day. It takes about four hours and entails taking a ferry across the Tejo (Tagus) river to the Barreiro station. There is also a stopping train that runs between Lagos and Vila Real de Santo António. You must have a valid ticket before you travel; failure to do so will result in a fine.

SENIOR CITIZENS

Senior citizens (those over 65 years of age) need only pay 50 per cent of the fare when travelling on the Portuguese Railway (CP). Low-cost flight-only deals are available, and it is often possible to rent a villa or apartment for an extended winter stay for a fraction of the high season price. Hotels, too, offer extremely attractive rates to elderly people staying for several weeks at a time.

British-style telephone kiosk

STUDENT AND YOUTH TRAVEL

There are various schemes that enable young people to travel at a discount. An InterRail card allows persons under 26 unlimited second-class rail travel throughout most of Europe and Morocco for one month.

EuRail is a similar, slightly more expensive, scheme for non-Europeans. In Portugal it is possible to obtain reduced train fares by travelling on 'blue days', off-peak periods. Further details can be obtained from the information desk of Santa Apolonia station, Lisbon (tel: (01) 876025/877092).

Holders of an International Student Card, International Youth Card or an International Teachers' Card are entitled to a variety of discounts including travel and museum entry. Cards can be obtained from Youth Travel Agencies. An International Youth Hostel Card will allow access to 18 hostels in Portugal. In the south there are hostels in the Alentejo at Portalegre and in the Algarve at Alcoutim, Vila Real de Santo António, Portimão and Sagres.

TELEPHONES

The best way to telephone abroad is from a post office. After queuing for a booth, the clerk times your call and you pay when you have finished.

Public kiosks that take phone cards are becoming increasingly more common, but if you use a phone in a hotel or a bar be prepared to pay a surcharge.

For international calls, dial 00 followed by the country code (Australia 61, Canada and the USA 1, Ireland 353 and the UK 44). Local calls can be made from coin boxes that accept 20 or 50 *escudos*.

Waiting for the bus

TIME

Portugal observes Greenwich Mean Time in the winter (from the last Sunday in September to the last Sunday in March). Clocks then go forward by one hour for the summer. Thus in summer, Portugal is five hours ahead of Eastern Standard Time and eight hours ahead of Pacific Time. South Africa is ahead by two hours, Australia by nine hours and New Zealand by 12.

TIPPING

Most hotel and restaurant bills include a service charge; a small tip (10 per cent) for a meal, taxi or for hotel staff who have helped you will be appreciated, but is not essential.

TOILETS

Public toilets are not common, except at railway stations and main bus stations. The facilities of a bar or restaurant can

Ubiquitous Algarvian souvenirs

be used whether you are a customer or not. Facilities in the country may be a little primitive so it is well to take your own toilet tissue.

Doors are rather confusingly marked *Senhores* (men) and *Senhoras* (women), but they usually have a pictorial symbol to aid the perplexed.

TOURIST INFORMATION

Every main town in Portugal has a local tourist office (*Posto, Commissão de Turismo* or *Turismo*) which serves as an indispensable source of detailed information about local events and facilities. Not only will it provide you with free maps and leaflets (including timetables) but it will also give you a list of accommodation and restaurants. Nearly all tourist offices have an English-speaking member of staff.

The main office in the Algarve is at Faro: Região de Turismo do Algarve, Rua da Misericórdia 8 (tel: 089 803604).

Other main offices are:
Albufeira, Rua 5 de Outubro (tel: 089 585279);
Évora, Praça do Giraldo (tel: 066 22671);
Lagos, Largo Marques de Pombal (tel: 082 763031);
Loulé, Rua D Paio Peres Carreia (tel: 089 463900);
Portimão, Largo 1 de Dezembro (tel: 082 41913).

Thomas Cook offices

Star Vigens S.A. is the Thomas Cook representative in the Algarve. Branches are located at: Travessa Escola Araujo 31, Lisbon; and 1250 Lisboa Avenida dos Alidos, Porto.

As well as offering a full leisure travel service these branches can make coach, ferry and hotel reservations. The hire of cars and local holiday homes can be arranged, as can local tours. The branches also deal with passport and visa formalities and give away free maps of the Algarve. They are open from Monday to Friday.

ACKNOWLEDGEMENTS
The Automobile Association wishes to thank the following photographers and libraries for their assistance in the preparation of this book.

JERRY EDMANSON was commissioned to take all the pictures for the book except for the following.
STUART ABRAHAM 43a, 43b, 48a, 48b, 48c, 49a, 49b, 83, 129a, 143, 147, 182 .
J ALLAN CASH PHOTOLIBRARY 13, 19, 54/5a, 54/5b, 69, 76a, 76b, 77a, 77b, 77c, 105a, 105b, 113, 115b, 115c, 132, 133a, 157a, 158, 160a, 160b, 161.
SARAH ANDERSON 23a, 37, 41, 126.
NATURE PHOTOGRAPHERS LTD 127a (Andrew J Cleave), 127b (Kevin Carlson), 127c (Kevin Carlson), 135a (Paul Sterry), 135b (Brinsley Burbidge).
SPECTRUM COLOUR LIBRARY 20, 21a, 119a, 119b, 145, 146, 151, 152, 159.
WORLD PICTURES front cover
ZEFA PICTURE LIBRARY (UK) LTD 115a, 144a, 144b, 157b.
All the remaining photographs are in The Automobile Association's own picture library and were taken by Malcolm Birkitt, and Alex Kouprianoff (spine).

CONTRIBUTORS
Series Adviser: Melissa Shales   **Copy Editor:** Christopher Catling   **Indexer:** Marie Lorimer
Thanks to **Chris and Melanie Rice** for their updating work on this revised edition.